Praise for
Prodigals

"Greg Taylor opens up Jesus's story of the son returned from the far country in a way you've never seen it opened before. He makes room for all of us in the younger son's story. Our wanderings, our self-deceptions, our restlessness, our prodigality. Most of all, we see the Father's love and, through it, how to find home."

—**Leonard Allen,** Dean of the College of Bible and Ministry, Lipscomb University, and author of *Poured Out*

"Greg's book is a vulnerable and thoughtful exploration of each sentence in the story of the prodigal. His writing is so honest that I was invited into the same kind of honesty about my own place in Jesus's powerful parable."

—**Sara Gaston Barton,** Pepperdine University Chaplain and author of *A Woman Called*

"Broken heartedness and rejection, especially when dealt through misguided faith by friends or loved ones, carry a pain that is both traumatizing and spiritually confusing. However, God's grace, as exhibited by the father who welcomed back his prodigal son, is an anthem that can shatter the years, and even decades, of deep-recessed, soul-scarring pain. Greg Taylor's book reminds us that heart-wrenching hurt is nothing new in the world. What is new is our continued rediscovery of God's grace, which, like the eternal home he has prepared for each of us, has no end. Thank you, Greg, for the reminder that all of us are lost but are capable of being found again."

—**Andy Taylor,** editor, *Montgomery County Chronicle*

"I'm a prodigal. You're a prodigal. We're all prodigals. Greg's latest book firmly but graciously reminds us of our prodigal nature; but unlike so many authors who have interpreted this most significant parable, Greg will help you find your way home."

—**Dr. Jack R. Shock,** Distinguished Professor of Communication, Harding University

"In a time when so many are feeling lost, Greg Taylor's patient examination of the Prodigal Son parable is a timely reminder that Jesus is in the business of finding those who are lost and welcoming home all of us who are prodigal sons and daughters."

—**Amy Bost-Henegar,** pastor, preacher, chaplain

"Greg has personally lavished God's prodigal love on me by giving this Cerebral Palsied minister of the gospel my first published writing, which mobilized me to write a book. Now, Greg Taylor does not let you miss out on God's generous love like the younger prodigal wastes his fortune. I say 'younger' because my heart and mind are transformed by these pages. I see prodigal living in each person in this relevant story, including me. This mind-altering book destroys the 'us' and 'them' mentality. I'm now mobilized by rediscovering the prodigal love and grace of God. God has been prodigal, lavishly generous with his love to us all! Greg shows us how. I'm so thankful for this critical life-giving resource on my twenty-five-year-old ministry bookshelf."

—**Todd Lollar,** Founder of Mobilize Ministries, author of *Weak Is the New Strong: God's Perfect Power in You*

"Greg somehow manages to both call out my natural older brother tendencies and reveal there's more younger brother in me than I care to admit, while also challenging me to become more like the extravagant father who makes this story worth telling in the first place."

—**Wade Hodges,** Lead Minister, Greenville Oaks Church of Christ

"As someone who comes from a Christian family, I thoroughly enjoyed reading about the well-known parable of the prodigal son from a refreshingly unique perspective. From revelations about mission trips in Uganda to how faith impacts family relationships, *Prodigals* honestly and transparently portrays the experiences of a man who wants others to take an introspective journey."

—**Deon Osborne,** Managing Editor for *The Black Wall Street Times*

"Greg's use of the chapter headings as a way to walk through the parable was masterful. Beautiful. Perfect. His personal stories were so enjoyable and were lovely glimpses of faithfulness. The message I came away with is this: We are not gatekeepers of the kingdom of God; only messengers. God behaves how God behaves, and if God welcomes the prodigal, praise be to God—for I am the prodigal."

—**Brent Abney**

Prodigals

Prodigals

Finding Home When We've Lost the Way

GREG ROSS TAYLOR

LEAFWOOD
PUBLISHERS
an imprint of Abilene Christian University Press

PRODIGALS

Finding Home When We've Lost the Way

LEAFWOOD
PUBLISHERS
an imprint of Abilene Christian University Press

ISBN 978-1-68426-309-7

Printed in the United States of America

Cataloging-in-Publication Data is on file at the Library of Congress, Washington, DC.

Cover design by Thinkpen Design, LLC
Interior text design by Sandy Armstrong, Strong Design

Leafwood Publishers is an imprint of Abilene Christian University Press
ACU Box 29138
Abilene, Texas 79699

1-877-816-4455
www.leafwoodpublishers.com

23 24 25 26 27 28 29 / 7 6 5 4 3 2 1

For Ashley, Anna, and Jacob

Contents

Foreword by the Author's Son

As the only son of my father, the youngest child, and a first-time father of a son myself, it seems proper for me to write a foreword to his book about prodigal sons. But it would be amiss to neglect that this book is about prodigal daughters too. My sisters, even though they *told me* to write it and will edit me if I go astray, have just as much right to reflect on Jesus's famous parable and comment on our dad's book. This book is about all of us as prodigals on our way back home—even if we never left it!

My dad's take on the parable is unusual and worth deeply contemplating. Humanity has lost its way, and *Prodigals* is about Jesus's way of guiding us back home. In this book, you'll find more than thoughts and stories. You'll encounter the confessions of my dad, who shares his own flaws and even some of our family's faults. His confessions invite you into confessing also. So, here's my confession of my own prodigal ways symbolized by a story of sibling car wrecks.

My sisters had both gotten into fender benders by the time I learned how to drive. The older one hit the side of the garage, eliciting reactionary words from my parents that I had never heard before! The younger topped that by backing into the garage door from inside on an early morning. A few years later, I didn't make it much further down the road before rear-ending another car.

My wreck came at a particular moment of pride during my senior year on the same day I was to receive an academic award. I wanted to succeed where others had failed or fallen short, in everything—especially something as easy-peasy as driving without a record. In a word, I wanted to be perfect. And so far, I thought I had at least managed the facade, though I knew it was false from within.

When I rear-ended the car of two brothers, varsity soccer players, in front of our high school, I did the natural thing I never wanted to have to do in this situation: I called my dad. Even though it was a little fender bender, it was big for me. Dad seemed to arrive instantly, with kindness in his eyes. That day of one of my failures, my dad was there for me. He helped me work out the situation with the police who arrived soon, and he navigated all the insurance headache for me; but most importantly, he was there for me to hug me, hold me, and forgive me. He let me know how okay it was to make that mistake, to make any mistake, and to bounce back with newfound humility and grace.

In moments of failure, some more traumatic than a car wreck, I wanted to be received by my father who forgives me, and I wanted to learn how I could receive myself in that way of grace too. My dad taught me over and over that I would have to learn to imitate God's perfection not by striving to be perfect through self-righteousness, nor through an inward-facing gaze of judgment, but rather by being "merciful, just as your Father is merciful" (Luke 6:36) and practicing how I was loved and forgiven by giving those gifts away to others. I think that is the perfect lesson for a father to teach, maybe the lesson that a father *must teach* if he is to be a good father.

My dad does not so much teach lessons in this book as he does confess being a prodigal himself. He reads the parable as a fellow prodigal. For a son, this realization that my dad knows he is also a prodigal is revelatory and life changing. His approach got me thinking about the parable and wanting to confess here in a similar way.

When my dad began researching for this book, he shared Henri Nouwen's *Return of the Prodigal Son* with me, and I began seeing the ways I was more like the elder son than the younger. Just like with the car wreck, I am often puffed up by the false idea that I can be better than others if I don't make the same mistakes they do. What a horrible place that puts you in when you make them! In reading the parable again along with Nouwen's study, I saw myself in the way the elder son judges the younger brother's sins, turning his "loose" or "wild living" into "this son of yours who has squandered your property with prostitutes" (Luke 15:30). I also learned that Jesus addresses the parable to the Pharisees, the ultimate elder siblings of Israel, and the arch judges of others' sins. Similarly, they accuse Jesus of eating with sinners, the younger sons of Israel, which he did and still does, thank God! When I began to identify my inner self with the older son and the Pharisees, I learned my spiritual labor now must include weeding out the self-righteousness that comes from religious vainglory over my brothers and sisters.

I am biased, but Nouwen is not as funny as my dad. My favorite imaginations of this parable are filled with some of the goofiness that could only come from him. For starters, I always have pictured the younger son not merely wishing to but actually eating out of the pig trough. And by my dad's influence, I have often pictured the father, in saying, "all that is mine is yours," as sacrificing his very own warmth, comfort, and clothing to give his sons a total gift of himself, down to the very tunic off his back to save them.

What is most important is not whether we are the younger or the older prodigal, for we may always identify ourselves as some mixture of both. What matters is what God does for us whether we are down on our luck or high on our horse. In going back to examine the story again, I am most struck by what can only be the finest description of divine love apart from the cross. For this story is not just of prodigal children but ultimately of the Prodigal Father, who of infinite love and blessedness showers us in his loving-kindness. He is the Father with a prodigious love, who extravagantly celebrates our return to him, lavishes us, and does unnecessarily good and beautiful things like robe and ring us before the most sublime feast of his grace.

Thinking of two siblings in a story reminds me of those brothers who got out of the car I hit that day in front of school. My facade was shattered. I could make the same mistakes as my sisters! But the brothers were not angry. They were merciful with me too. Though I was a nervous, crying mess, they were sorry I hit their car and had to endure that kind of morning as well! As my dad says after each of our wrecks: "It is just metal and plastic, but what happens to your heart after this is what is most important." I have been in two more severe car accidents since then (one in my late grandpa's Cadillac) and have taken that phrase to heart after each.

Whether we are the younger, the older, or both, our merciful Father says to us: *Child, you are always with me, and all that is mine is yours*. However your life mixes and matches the elder and the younger, the Mary and the Martha, in your life, this is your story, all our stories, because it is the Father's story of Prodigal Love. I am so happy, very pleased, overly delighted to be blabbering a toast to introduce my good father's interpretations, ideas, and imaginations about this, Jesus's best, story.

Jacob Ross Taylor

Prologue

My parents are legendary in my Oklahoma hometown. Born during the depression, they did not know a stranger. They never ate a Sunday dinner alone. If you were a drifter wandering into church, you would get invited to the Taylor home. Dad built the house. Mom set the table with food that attracted neighbors and strangers. One Sunday, so many came for lunch that Dad carried them all to the house in the church bus.

Mom and Dad had two boys and two girls, a perfect family symmetry; then they had me. We all knew we could invite our friends to eat or stay with us. My best friends, Brooks and Brian, invited themselves to wedge in on my share of Mom's locally famous cinnamon rolls. (I ate my weight at their moms' kitchens as well, so it all averaged out.)

After my siblings and I moved from home, Mom would write us letters, telling us about how Jeff was living in my old room. I don't know who Jeff is. Mom would bake and send Jeff with a batch of cinnamon rolls, and Dad would see to it that he or someone in town would give Jeff a job. They housed many Jeffs.

Because Mom and Dad were a one-family restaurant-and-temp-job service, they were not satisfied with starting the most successful home-building business in our town. In the seventies, when I was growing up, they started a diner called The Buffeteria.

Dad went in for breakfast one day and the manager said they were getting overrun with business. Dad checked the register and it had rung up fourteen bucks in sales. Getting overrun like that was going to run them right out of business. Then he had the pancakes. Fork by fork, bathed in syrup, Dad kept tasting soap in that stack of hotcakes. He went to the kitchen to ask the cook how he made them. Everything was good right up to the point where he added water, from the auto soap dispenser in the dish-washing station.

The Buffeteria buffeted right on out of business in less than a year, but the good news is that Dad always wanted to start a used car lot. Every business Mom and Dad ran was calculated to provide people in town with jobs, a better life, and something to drive. I had left my 1980 Dodge Colt station wagon at home when at college one semester. You cannot just park a car and let the battery run down, right? Dad's solution was to give my car to Jeff.

Mom and Dad are not legendary because of homes, cars, and soapy pancakes. They are legendary because they seemed to know and live out the mysteries of the greatest parable Jesus ever told. That parable has long been titled "The Prodigal Son." How did Mom and Dad cut through misleading ways of telling this parable that have chopped up the world into prodigals and non-prodigals? The quest to bring the parable out of centuries of lockdown and discover its mysteries has motivated five years of biblical research, art exploration, writing, and discussions with Mom and Dad, my siblings, my wife, and my children.

Each chapter of this book explores a sentence in the parable Jesus tells. Getting face-to-face like this with the characters, I discovered a key to reading the parable. I am reading and commenting on the parable as a fellow prodigal. As you read and engage with me in a few thoughts on each line of the story, can you begin to see yourself in the characters? For future editions of this book, I hope you will consider sending me a prodigal story of your own to letters@prodigals.me.

The Story Told by Jesus

Luke 15:1–32

Now the tax collectors and sinners were all gathering around to hear Jesus. But the Pharisees and the teachers of the law muttered, "This man welcomes sinners and eats with them."

Then Jesus told them this parable: "Suppose one of you has a hundred sheep and loses one of them. Doesn't he leave the ninety-nine in the open country and go after the lost sheep until he finds it? And when he finds it, he joyfully puts it on his shoulders and goes home. Then he calls his friends and neighbors together and says, 'Rejoice with me; I have found my lost sheep.' I tell you that in the same way there will be more rejoicing in heaven over one sinner who repents than over ninety-nine righteous persons who do not need to repent.

Or suppose a woman has ten silver coins and loses one. Doesn't she light a lamp, sweep the house and search carefully until she finds it? And when she finds it, she calls her friends and neighbors together and says, 'Rejoice with me; I have found my lost coin.' In the same way, I tell you, there is rejoicing in the presence of the angels of God over one sinner who repents."

"There was a man who had two sons. The younger one said to his father, 'Father, give me my share of the estate.' So he divided his property between them.

Not long after that, the younger son got together all he had, set off for a distant country and there squandered his wealth in wild living. After he had spent everything, there was a severe famine in that whole country, and he began to be in need. So he went and hired himself out to a citizen of that country, who sent him to his fields to feed pigs. He longed to fill his stomach with the pods that the pigs were eating, but no one gave him anything.

When he came to his senses, he said, 'How many of my father's hired servants have food to spare, and here I am starving to death! I will set out and go back to my father and say to him: Father, I have sinned against heaven and against you. I am no longer worthy to be called your son; make me like one of your hired servants.' So he got up and went to his father.

But while he was still a long way off, his father saw him and was filled with compassion for him; he ran to his son, threw his arms around him and kissed him.

The son said to him, 'Father, I have sinned against heaven and against you. I am no longer worthy to be called your son.'

But the father said to his servants, 'Quick! Bring the best robe and put it on him. Put a ring on his finger and sandals on his feet. Bring the fattened calf and kill it. Let's have a feast and celebrate. For this son of mine was dead and is alive again; he was lost and is found.' So they began to celebrate.

Meanwhile, the older son was in the field. When he came near the house, he heard music and dancing. So he called one of the servants and asked him what was going on. 'Your brother has come,' he replied, 'and your father has killed the fattened calf because he has him back safe and sound.'

The older brother became angry and refused to go in. So his father went out and pleaded with him. But he answered his father, 'Look! All these years I've been slaving for you and never disobeyed your orders. Yet you never gave me even a young goat so I could celebrate with my friends. But when this son of yours who has squandered your property with prostitutes comes home, you kill the fattened calf for him!'

'My son,' the father said, 'you are always with me, and everything I have is yours. But we had to celebrate and be glad, because this brother of yours was dead and is alive again; he was lost and is found.'"

1

Sons

There was a man who had two sons.

My Grandpa Ross was a man of few words. He figured Grandma Grace had used their family's daily allotment of words by breakfast. One day at their barn, I was breaking the ice for the cows and horses. But I made a mistake: I left the gate open. Two horses wandered out and onto the road. One horse bolted toward the nearby state highway. Grandpa grabbed a bucket of feed, and with the help of neighbors, we coaxed the horses back to the safety of the corral. When Grandpa was aggravated, he whinnied like a frustrated horse. He neighed at me a few times that day.

Our neighbors called my grandparents Amazing Grace and Old Rugged Ross. I loved Grandpa Ross and Grandma Grace, who lovingly helped raise me and teach me to ranch, garden, and sit on the porch swing listening to the birds sing while twiddling our thumbs.

My grandparents fell victim, however, to a narrow and harmful interpretation of this beloved parable of Jesus. Many churches, preachers, and teachers have told the greatest story of Jesus in such a way that hearers like my grandparents were ready to divide the world—even their families—between the faithful and the prodigals. Could it be that the most popular interpretation of this parable has been badly bungled? Here's how such an interpretation of the parable impacted my family.

My grandparents had two sons, my dad and my uncle Rudy. One day when Rudy was an adult, he used a new translation of the Bible to teach a class in the small Kansas-town church where my grandfather was an elder. The other elders decided this version was not authorized and took over Rudy's teaching responsibilities. One elder's way of teaching the class was to say that the old half of the Bible did not matter. The takeover of his class and the misleading teaching led my uncle and his family to attend a church up the road.

The fallout was swift: my grandpa, humiliated, resigned as elder, believing he was no longer qualified because his youngest son had "left the truth." Many families understand what it is like to have conflict with their relatives. When my uncle would visit his parents, tension filled the air. Normal things that would ordinarily be reasons for celebration—like the time he told his parents he had baptized his children—became awkward. My grandparents could only return blank stares, silence, and whispers of grave concern. They were now worried not only about their son's eternal state but their grandchildren's as well.

Meanwhile, Uncle Rudy and Aunt Kathy served for decades at that church up the road. A woman at their church once told my uncle he could be thankful his parents cared enough to take a stand, even if wrongly handled. He said he holds no grudges—just grief for what was lost. There is much lost in many families that take an excluding line against prodigals in their own families. I am not claiming my read on the parable is the only one or even the right one. But I want to excavate and reexamine interpretations of the Bible in general and this parable in particular that do harm to people.

The story Jesus tells opens with the classic line, "There was a man who had two sons." The first surprise of the story is that Jesus calls neither son prodigal. *Prodigal* does not appear in the text of the parable. Someone titled the story "The Prodigal Son" as a heading in one Bible translation, and it has since appeared in others. *Prodigal* is a mysterious word, because it can mean wasteful, lavish, and excessive in negative or positive ways. Most often, however, rule makers use *prodigal* to describe those they think are stinkers.

Luke is the only biblical writer who tells this story of the man who had two sons. Luke puts the story together with two other parables. One common theme in each of the parables is lost and found things.

My wife's grandmother, Ma Rudd, went to Russia and brought back wooden nesting dolls. You open two halves of the large doll, and there is a smaller doll inside. Repeat this a half-dozen times until there is the tiniest doll that cannot open. Like Russian nesting dolls, Luke nests these three parables inside the context of Jesus interacting with religious opposition, and that subplot nests inside the life story of Jesus.

Interestingly, it was people who knew they were sinners who had gathered to hear Jesus tell stories. The religion teachers muttered under their breath, "This man welcomes sinners and eats with them" (Luke 15:2). Jesus decided the religious people needed to stay for story time and began telling a series of three parables.

The first of the three stories is about a shepherd who loses a lamb. He has a hundred sheep, and the shepherd leaves the ninety-nine to search for one lost lamb. When the shepherd finds the lamb, he calls his friends together and they celebrate. To the stubborn religious folks with folded arms, Jesus brings the message home: "In the same way there will be more rejoicing in heaven over one sinner who repents than over ninety-nine righteous persons who do not need to repent" (v. 7).

The second story is about a woman who has ten coins, and one goes missing. Can't we all relate to the stress of losing a wallet, phone, keys? She wastes no time and lights a lantern, sweeps the whole house, and, whoa yeah, she finds it! Can't we all relate to the joy of finding those lost keys?! She calls her neighbors over and says, "Let's party! I had lost a coin but have found it!" A second time Jesus says, "I tell you, there is rejoicing in the presence of the angels of God over one sinner who repents" (v. 10).

These two parables set up the longest of the three stories, the one about a man who had two sons. An important thing to remember for now is that these opening words signal that the story is not only about one son, not about one prodigal. There are other visible and off-screen characters in the story who are also prodigals.

Hebrew scholar Amy-Jill Levine says the first line, "a man who had two sons," recalls other pairs of siblings in the Hebrew Bible.[1] In the story of creation, Adam and Eve had two sons. Their story is humanity's story of jealous rage, murder, family shame, and resilience. Cain is jealous of Abel and kills him. "Then the Lord said to Cain, 'Where is your brother Abel?' 'I don't know,' [Cain] replied. 'Am I my brother's keeper?'" (Gen. 4:9). Recalling other stories may add depth to the parable, leading us to wonder: Did the brothers in the parable question whether they were their brother's keeper? Do you and I?

First hearers of the story may have also thought of Isaac and Ishmael, Leah and Rachel, Jacob and Esau. Each of their stories unfold like reality shows, with people vying for family property and blessings. These are a few of the stories the first hearers and we may remember when we hear the first line of the parable. Reading the Bible "rightly" is not always about finding answers or justification for our ways of life or doctrines; it can also be about asking more heart-changing questions of ourselves. So when it comes to remembering these other family pairs, we might ask questions that touch our lives today. For example, I wonder, Are family blessings a zero-sum game? Does one child have to be blessed and the other unblessed?

I never imagined the story of the prodigal son was being played out in my own family. I suppose this is a bit of frustrated whinnying of my own, but my grandpa misled our extended family to not acknowledge the faith of my uncle and his family. Grandpa and his fellow elders had been confused by questionable Bible teaching that marginalizes prodigals and believes God's blessings and salvation are limited to one brand of Christian church. This is one way that trying to "rightly divide the word of truth" is misleading and can negatively impact people. When my grandparents moved away from Kansas to my small Oklahoma town, they built a house and barn next door to their older son, his wife, and their five children. I was the youngest of those five children, and I did not realize the reasons for my grandparents' move were related to their sense of shame over their younger son leaving their church. At the time, I never imagined my gain of my grandparents living next door would be my cousins' loss. My cousin Andy told me that while seeing our grandparents leave his hometown in Kansas to live in my Oklahoma hometown was sad, his family's move to another church was the best thing his parents could have done. He and his siblings grew up in a loving and faith-nurturing church community.

I am making my own mistakes, as you will see in stories I tell in this book. I do not, however, want to generationally repeat the response of my grandparents not affirming the faith of their children and grandchildren. After growing up in Protestant Christian churches, my youngest child, Jacob, and his wife, Sidney, decided to be confirmed as Catholics. In an age group that statistically attends church the least, I respect the faithfulness Jacob and Sidney have to God and to their worshipping community. What many Christians do not always realize is that there is a five-hundred-year-old rift between Catholic and Protestant churches. This rift often influences how Catholics and Protestants view and treat one another. Jacob and Sidney experienced a few negative responses from loved ones that were similar to responses my uncle and family received. As an affirming response, Jill and I attended Sidney and Jacob's confirmation in the Catholic Church on Easter. And we continue to have open conversations about what it means to be a family in communion while practicing faith in different ways.

My definition of a prodigal is anyone who accepts their sinful human nature and turns in repentance toward the love of home, the place where we find a deeper relationship with God. My primary definition of sin is any act of bodily, psychological-emotional, economic, and/or spiritual harm to another human being. Sin against humanity is also sin against the divine creator of humanity. Taking on a prodigal identity does not mean we excuse sin in ourselves or others. It means we take sinful harm of self, God, and others even more seriously. It also means we do what breaks the strongholds of sin in our prodigal hearts: loving and forgiving ourselves as God lavishly loves and forgives us; loving and forgiving fellow prodigals. I forgive and love my grandfather just as I love and forgive myself, for we are both prodigals. I believe my grandfather loves and forgives me for letting the horse out of the gate and this story outside of the family.

My grandfather and grandmother were prodigals. My father was a prodigal. My mother is a prodigal. I am a prodigal. My wife is a prodigal. My children are prodigals. We are all prodigals. Even you are a prodigal. Will you come to this parable of Jesus with me as a fellow prodigal? Maybe you have always viewed the parable as cutting the world into prodigals and non-prodigals. This is a misdirected way of reading into the parable something that has never been there. And this leads to choosing sides in all forms of life, including religion, politics, race, education, health, and geography. We don't have to read the parable that way.

How would life change if we began to lean in and learn a new identity, as prodigals? As we move deeper into the parable, can you begin to imagine how the parable is playing out in your life and family?

Prodigal Prayer

God, I want to tell stories that make me and my family look good. I don't want to reveal my own and my family's prodigal lives. Help me be as honest and transparent as I possibly can right now.

2

Mine

The younger one said to his father, "Father, give me my share of the estate."

The results of my straw poll are in. Parents should not let their teenagers sail on the ocean around the world alone. That is, unless the teen is Laura Dekker, who began a solo global voyage at fourteen years old. This while other teens navigate the choppy seas of high school.

When Laura proposed the idea to her father and mother, who had sailed some of the same routes before their divorce, they first thought she was crazy. She continued her pleading, and they gave way. They were not alone in their thinking she was taking an elevated risk. Fortunately, social media had been invented so that millions of armchair parents could weigh in on what they thought about the parents of the Dutch teenager circling the earth on the family's forty-foot sailboat, with no crew—and did I say she would be alone except for sixty pounds of mac and cheese? A court in

Holland even tried to stop the derelict Dekkers and take Laura into child protective custody.

Laura had been born on a sailboat and spent the first five years of her life sailing. She sailed a dingy daily, and she first sailed from Holland to Great Britain in a small sailing boat. Laura was more familiar with sailing on water than walking on land.

The courts did not stop her, and Laura began her voyage. She sailed in three oceans, around the horn of Africa in high winds and sixty-foot swells. She wasn't trying to be the fastest, just the youngest. She stopped along the way and enjoyed time with people, docking in places such as the Galapagos Islands and Durban, South Africa. When she completed the voyage, the world was amazed. In 2012, then sixteen-year-old Laura Dekker became the youngest person ever to sail around the world alone.

Just as there were many opinions about Laura Dekker's solo trip around the world, so there is no agreement about the wisdom or foolishness of a son asking for the family's prized property—in first-century Palestine or now. There is an early surprising twist to the story Jesus tells. Not just the son but the *younger* son asks for his rightful inheritance *before* his father's death.

For Laura Dekker's parents, their daughter's request to take the family's boat around the world seemed so natural. They'd taught Laura the routes, helped their daughter build the boat, installed navigational instruments, and of course stocked that mac and cheese. By freely receiving the tools and supplies she needed, Laura knew how to circle back toward home after a long and far journey. Her parents risked everything to give a form of living inheritance to Laura.

As in the story of Laura Dekker, it is easy to judge the actions of the father for giving away his inheritance. But what if the father had the same kind of response to his son as Laura's parents did to her request? The parents in both stories are freely giving an inheritance to their children.

Nothing in the parable suggests the son did anything wrong at this point by asking for his inheritance. I have heard preachers say the son asking for his inheritance would effectively say to the father, "I wish you dead." Preachers may be juicing the story here; and surely I would never do that, would I? There is no sign the son wished his father dead by asking for his part of the inheritance.

Can you imagine how the son feels living at home, wanting to see the world, sitting on wealth he cannot get his hands on, about to bust? He approaches the most trusted person in his life. The son makes a simple statement that will change his life forever. The words form less of a question than a demand. In English, there are four words, and 50 percent are "me" and "my."

The younger son says these four words to the father: "Give me my share."

Imagine that real family money or land is at stake and you want it badly. Someone else might get it; someone else might spoil what you want; someone else might use the money you need now for your college education, your child's life-saving surgery.

Chances are you can imagine just such a scenario, because rich and poor, people are vexed when wealth is at stake. If you need it and you feel you have some right to it, you ask, fight, connive, or sacrifice for the inheritance. It's the basis for many television, stage, and movie comedies and tragedies. Something of value is at stake. People are willing to do anything to get it. Many of us are closer to *Breaking Bad* than we might be willing to admit.

"There is no way she's going to let that gold digger marry her and take my inheritance away to a new in-law after all these years!"

"I deserve more than this. I'm getting ripped off. When I win the lottery, I'm going to buy a boat and sail away from all my troubles."

"Just give me the money now so that poser cannot have it!"

"Grandpa is sitting on all those oil and gas leases, and his grandchildren need college tuition money!"

"Give me my share . . ."

I remember in my twenties appealing to the notion of fairness for everyone when a competing motivation was getting my share. How does "give me my share" impact how I go about my daily interactions? Does jealousy crowd my thoughts of happiness when good things happen to other people? Do I hear myself saying "give me my share" of what I think I deserve?

I still wonder if those words the son said hurt the father. Were the words offensive? Why didn't the father rebuke the younger son? If there is any shame in the request, the father does not show it. Without offense, the father does something that surprises the first hearers of the story. If we come face-to-face with the characters in the parable, the father's response may surprise us, too.

3

Property

So he divided his property between them.

Dividing inheritance can blow up in family Armageddon. A Maryland couple, however, imagined a brilliant way to split family wealth without the family splitting up. The family even had fun divvying up possessions. *Washington Post* writer Thomas Heath tells the story of this couple who invited their adult sons and daughter to their home, gave them each two thousand dollars in play money, and announced they would conduct an auction for the family stuff.

One of the sons, David Landau, said his "friends fight with siblings over their parents' stuff—not the expensive stuff, but odds and ends that each child wanted. My [parents] avoided this problem brilliantly. Dad was the auctioneer and Mom recorded the results."[1]

Household artwork, furniture, and bobbleheads worth little money were bid up because they had special meaning to the adult siblings. Heath's article quotes wills-and-estates lawyer Tim Price, who says, "The best way to distribute your estate is while you are still alive."

With no plan for distribution of possessions, some families do not divvy up but blow up. For example, after a mother enters a nursing home, her son backs up a rental truck and empties her house. A sister takes her deceased mother's silverware before the siblings talk about it. Even the Landaus' family-friendly meeting had an edge to it.

"My brother wanted a living room chair that had belonged to my grandparents," David Landau remembered. "I knew my brother wanted that chair, so I purposely drove up the bidding. He said, 'You aren't playing fair.' I said: 'You are my younger brother. I never play fair.'"

What David really wanted was the Baltimore Colts bobblehead to remember the times he attended football games with his dad.

Ready to get out the play money and call the family together for an inheritance auction? The Landau family way of distributing family possessions is a hard no for most families. I don't imagine families in Palestine during Jesus's life would have pulled out the play money for such a "game." So, how *did* people react to this line in the story: "So he divided his property between them"? What's the Aramaic phrase for "What a nincompoop!"?

The younger son does not seem to know the extravagance of what he's asking, does not seem grateful. There is little indication in the parable, however, that the father pays attention to those things. The father seemed perfectly willing to divide his wealth and give the younger son his due part freely. There is no sign of resistance, scolding, or withholding of this rightful inheritance.

How much inheritance did the younger son receive? What form of capital was the inheritance in? Was it livestock, land, jewels, spices? Whatever the form, the inheritance soon became mobile for the son to take far away. The younger son may have received a third portion of the father's wealth. If you don't want to know the biblical math, then here's an equation for you. What was said in the story plus how much we know about first-century practices equals, we don't know how much the younger son got.

The irony of family wealth in this case is that it is the very thing that finances a trip away from the family. When our children were young, we sometimes appealed to money for motivation, sometimes negatively: "You are *not* going to act that way while you spend my money!" Please do not take this or any of my parenting quotes as sound parenting models. I've not always put my best paw forward.

Ruth Bell Graham tells a story about a son who turned his back on his father's faith. Knowing he could not force his son to follow Jesus, the father said to his son, "That is your freedom, your terrible freedom."[2]

What will we do with this "terrible freedom"? Will we use it to finance our trip away from family or faith in God? Some people have a literal inheritance of money or land. Others may have a yet unnamed and underappreciated wealth of education, social, cultural, religious networks upon which they can build lives if they so choose. Still others have no literal inheritance but trust in what the apostle Peter called "an inheritance which is imperishable, undefiled, and unfading, kept in heaven for you" (1 Pet. 1:4 RSV).

American philosopher and activist Cornel West challenges those who have been recipients of wealth to discern whether these are true blessings of God or sinfully acquired benefits.[3] Often Americans get locked into a false dichotomy between, "I worked hard to earn what I have!" and "We have a responsibility to help others." Could it be possible that someone has worked hard but also feels responsible to help others?

Wealth does not always indicate that a person has really worked hard, nor is it a sign of faithfulness. We can witness unfaithful and faithful rich persons just as we can witness faithful and unfaithful poor persons. As much as we like to have it both ways, however, Jesus lays the heaviest responsibility on rich people. It is the rich, not the poor, who most need to discern where they have acquired their wealth, how to offload it to help low-income families, and how to live humbly without thinking it was skills and goodness that got them this far.

I just used third person "they" to describe rich people. That's how most of us do it—we think rich are "they." Compared to half the world making a few dollars a day, however, all of us who live in a home, drive a car, and have some cash in our pockets are rich. I know, I do not understand your situation. I get it. But you are likely richer than most of the world's population.

Rich people were put off by Jesus's radical statements that they should give away their wealth to the poor and follow him. There was a wealthy man, however, who impressed Jesus by a crazy public pledge he made about his possessions. We sing a song about this man to children in church. While we busy ourselves with this song that redundantly offends this "wee little man," we have missed a powerful ending and affirmation by Jesus the song never mentions.

There was once a man named Zacchaeus who lived in Jericho. I imagine he looked and talked like Vizzini the Sicilian in *The Princess Bride*. He was everyone's favorite guy in the neighborhood: a tax collector. One day when Jesus of Nazareth came to his town, he climbed a tree to see him because, being stubby like me, he could not see over the crowds. For some reason Jesus singled out Zacchaeus and said, "Come down, for I'm going to your house today." This is usually where the children's song stops and as far as our knowledge of the story has gone. But Luke 19:7–10 narrates the rest of the story:

> All the people saw this and began to mutter, "He has gone to be the guest of a sinner."
>
> But Zacchaeus stood up and said to the Lord, "Look, Lord! Here and now I give half of my possessions to the poor, and if I have cheated anybody out of anything, I will pay back four times the amount."
>
> Jesus said to him, "Today salvation has come to this house, because this man, too, is a son of Abraham. For the Son of Man came to seek and to save the lost."

What was this crazy commitment of Zacchaeus that prompted Jesus to say, "Salvation has come to this house"? The biblical idea of restitution is likely what Zacchaeus was drawing from, except he upped the scale by many times. Zacchaeus committed to giving away half of his wealth to the poor. He also committed to repay four times restitution if he'd defrauded anyone. Today we call this restorative justice or reparations. Many followers of Jesus today have never considered reparations as a part of Christian faith. Yet reparations are a biblically inspired action about which Jesus praises God and says, "Salvation has come to this house."

Like the father in Jesus's parable, Zacchaeus freely offers up a sizable portion of family wealth. Zacchaeus was not using play money. While he was living, he divided his wealth not with his own family but with poor community members and to anyone he'd defrauded. Watching this outrageous turn of events, were Zacchaeus's wife and children on board or biting their knuckles? What happened in the next years with Zacchaeus's family? Those could have been the most blessed and beautiful years in their lifetimes.

They may have even given away the family bobblehead.

Prodigal Prayer

God, I realize I have inherited so many things, including the ways of sin. I need your prodigious grace to confront how evil has schemed its way into my life and my ancestors' lives. When you have revealed wicked ways against my neighbors, grant me humility and show me merciful actions to take like Zacchaeus to reconcile with them.

4

Far

Not long after that, the younger son got together all he had, set off for a distant country . . .

I was seventeen when I left my hometown in Oklahoma to see the world! I got as far as Arkansas. At a Christian college, I became a self-appointed watchdog for righteousness in the freshmen dorm. For example, I once removed a poster from a hallmate's wall without his knowledge, then asked a suitemate to lie and keep my secret. He did, for a few minutes. When the owner of the poster arrived in my room, he was livid. I explained that the poster included a mild sexual innuendo. The poster's owner, an exceptionally large football player, wanted to know: *Who was I to steal in the name of morality?* Good point. *And wasn't I also mildly fascinated with sex as well?* Another good point. But this was a Christian college!

I was such a watchdog for righteousness that I thought I already knew the Bible. When I took college Bible courses, I already knew what professors were teaching, so why take notes? Before the final, however, I extorted notes from my girlfriend. This would not be the last time my girlfriend, who later became my wife, would deal with my prodigality in the form of lazy, stubborn pride.

At nineteen, I went even further from home. I joined forty fellow college students for a trip overseas. For most of us, it was the first time we'd left our home country. The experience of traveling to Amsterdam for pizza, Italy for pizza, and France for pizza opened my mind and expanded my waistline. I have a pin map of the world on the wall in front of me as I write. Simply by looking at the pins, I can be teleported in my mind's eye to the farthest points on the Earth that I've traveled. Like Samwise Gamgee in *The Lord of the Rings*, I know just how many steps I've taken out of the Shire. When you go beyond the Shire, every step you take is the furthest you've been from home.

Something similar happens when training for a marathon. As I roll up the miles and training runs get longer, each training run is the longest I've ever run. Finally running a marathon, with each step past my twenty-two-mile training run I thought, *This is the farthest I've ever run at one time.* I only ran one marathon, so this is a one-time humble brag—for this chapter anyway.

The parable includes the detail that after asking for his inheritance, "a few days passed." Was the unseen mother in the story pleading for her son to stay? Did anyone get sleep those few nights? To neighbors and family, news of the younger son's leaving would have traveled before he did. The neighbors might have known because the son may have visited them with a string of goats to liquidate the inheritance into something more spendable. There are no online bookings, hastily packed suitcases, or squealing tires in this story.

My oldest daughter, my wife, and I have a February tradition of watching that year's Oscar-nominated films. I'm not just talking about the best picture films but also the animated shorts, documentary shorts, and live-action shorts that play at the art house Circle Cinema in Tulsa, Oklahoma, where we live. We're geeks, we know. One year we saw a French film called *Negative Space*, a 2017 Oscar-nominated short, stop-motion, animated film directed by Ru Kuwahata and Max Porter.

A boy learns from his father how to pack a suitcase, rolling shirts and filling the space perfectly so everything stays right where he packed it. The father goes on many trips, and the son always packs for his father. Years pass, the boy packs his own bag now, and moves away. The father grows old and dies. At the funeral, the now grown son observes his father's corpse with extra space in the casket. The son narrates the last line of the short, animated movie: "The funeral was terrible. My dad laid out in that big carton. And me thinking, *Look at all that wasted space*."

In a world where we can travel very far, very fast, going to a faraway country does not seem odd to us in the least. When the younger son set out for a distant country, however, he was doing more than "seeing the world." As the late Catholic priest Henri Nouwen writes, the small detail that the younger son "left for a distant country" indicates a "cutting loose" from the father's way of life. He rejects the sacred family traditions. By going far away, the son does not only forego the pleasure of family gatherings. Traveling to a distant country may have also signaled a wholesale rejection of the family's traditions, religion, food, and lifestyle.

As I've read this parable for years, Nouwen, who wrote *The Return of the Prodigal Son*, has been my Obi-Wan. Like a Padawan, I am being apprenticed by the powerful force of this parable for life change. For example, my mentor ponders in what ways the faraway country is preferred to his spiritual home: "But when I forget that voice of the first unconditional love, then these innocent suggestions can easily start dominating my life and pull me into the 'distant country.' It is not very hard for me to know when this is happening. Anger, resentment, jealousy, desire for revenge, lust, greed, antagonisms, and rivalries are the obvious signs that I have left home."[1]

Other theologians get symbolic and spiritual mileage out of this idea of the son traveling to "a distant country." In Church Father Augustine's own story, he traveled far from home in selfish and sinful pursuits, and after several years he returned home. He alludes to his prodigal nature in his *Confessions*. For example, his "distant country" was not only a place far from home but a state of mind far from God. When Augustine's best friend died he was inconsolable. He wondered if his abundance of grief for his friend betrayed a distance from God. C. S. Lewis had much love for Augustine, at least "four loves." He did not disagree with Augustine on much, but with fear and trembling, he did disagree with Augustine here. Lewis says diminishing our love for humans is not the best way to increase love for God. Whatever issue creates unhealthy distance between humans and God also puts negative space between humans.[2]

When I was a young adult, I traveled far, carrying some family ways, unpacking and leaving behind some family baggage. I do not claim that I am right and my family wrong. Some families, however, may take a child's leaving for a far country—leaving church, moving away, not running the family business—as an offense. My adult children have moved far and near to us. Though they carry some of our ways, they may be ready to travel far and shed some of our ways. I do not think my children are right or wrong in these decisions either. It is just too much of a moving target to always know, nor is it always important to know.

If you are a teenage reader, you have likely not left home yet—or maybe you are in foster care and know exactly what it's like to leave home, how painful or exciting. If you have left home before, chances are you felt a similar mix of exhilaration and anxiety of leaving home as I did. You did not want to leave. You wanted to leave. You dreaded the day you had to leave family. You could not wait to go. You were deeply sad. You were giddy with anticipation of the adventures ahead.

How far away from home have you traveled? What is your faraway country? Does your baggage have any negative space?

5

Squander

. . . and there squandered his wealth in wild living.

When I was twenty-five years old, my wife and I lived in Houston, Texas. Jill taught high school math. I was a youth minister. One day I was off work and getting gas in our 1981 Oldsmobile Cutlass Supreme. About the time I snapped the license plate back over the hidden gas cap in the back of the car, a man approached me.

The man said he was from Haiti. We were next to the airport. He asked for a ride to a car dealer a few miles away. He got in and as we drove, he spoke about selling his business in Haiti and his desire to settle here where his children lived. He wanted to buy a car to get where they lived. He had a roll of bills he showed me.

We arrived at a used car lot and a man approached to help us. I was ready to go when the man from Haiti showed his cash to the car dealer. The car salesman reacted and told the man not to flash his cash like that. At the time I was young, naïve, and had never been targeted for a scam. Now I had just been targeted by a man with a fake Haitian accent, a fake wad of cash, and a fake car dealer confidence man. I was off work, had time to chat, and was intrigued by the man's offer to pay me for helping him that day. I had five hundred dollars cash in my wallet for Christmas shopping. Through a series of slick talk and sleight of hand, one of the men slipped away with my wallet. When I went outside to look for him, I returned to find the other man gone as well.

I can still remember talking to Jill in the garage about what happened that day. By naïve and selfish motives, I had dumped our money in the garbage can. Now I had to tell the story to my wife. What is your spouse supposed to say when you have squandered five hundred dollars? How could I? What was I thinking? You cannot con an honest man.

The younger son in the parable went to a distant country and squandered his property in wild living. Another word some translations use here is "foolish" living. A lot of us who don't think we were the "wild child" get off easy thinking we're not prodigals, but let's see if the parable carries that water for us or if there are holes in that bucket. I am focusing in this chapter on a kind of foolishness where pride, selfishness, and naïveté lead to squandering. The elder brother later expounds on the younger son's "wild living" when he complains to the father how his brother has "squandered your property with prostitutes." I'll return to the older brother's accusation about the younger brother's sexual exploits in a later chapter.

The reason I've embarrassed myself again to tell you my story of getting conned is this: while many of us don't like to talk about our own foolishness, confessing we are not all-wise is healthy. I have told you only one of my squandering stories, and you are officially spared from reading any others. What if admitting our past or current squandering could teach us something vital for our lives?

Imagine a huge bank where you deposited squandered gifts, money, relationships, and gallons or pounds of too much of something you consumed. Let's call it the First National Bank of Squandered Gifts. What if we could visit FNBSG? You can enter the safety deposit room and see the deposits of squandered valuables. In a locked box are squandered relationships. In another box is squandered money, education, and all the time you spent playing Angry Birds. Would you like to visit that bank and withdraw that lost time, money, education, opportunities, and relationships?

What if that bank really did exist but all the time, we have been visiting the bank across town that is bankrupt? We keep returning to the rival bank that is filled with regrets, guilt, and shame. This International Bank of Guilt and Shame (IBGS) is charging us exorbitant interest on every transaction. We are looking for the bank where we have not burned a bridge, where it does not hurt, where we can continue to pretend we never made mistakes, where we can forget the pain we caused or someone caused us. The marketing is slick for this bank, but it sucks the life from us.

Imagine instead you can revisit FNBSG and withdraw wisdom in place of foolishness? A classic definition of *prodigal* is one who squanders family wealth, with no reference to whether the person has repented or not. A compact set of words describes what the younger son did and what I did in Houston on the streets that day. "Squandered. Property. Foolishly."

Take the word "property" in the parable and replace it with the thing you've squandered: time, money, relationships, education, opportunities. The question here is not so much, "Have you ever squandered anything?" We have all squandered something. The question is, "What are you going to learn from the squandering?" For example, I have helped lead in businesses, churches, and nonprofits, some which have closed. Closing does not necessarily mean failure, but feelings of failure and squandering often prevail in the minds of people who were involved in those organizations. We may not be able to withdraw wasted time, energy, and opportunities, but we most certainly can withdraw wisdom from the FNBSG.

I did not want to revisit my gullibility, but what if that visit to the FNBSG could provide wisdom in gullibility's place? For example, what if being conned saved my children's lives? Had I not learned this life lesson, in the future I might have been naïve enough to leave my child with a stranger at the grocery store while I dashed back to get some eggs. I learned a tough lesson about human nature. I had been a trusting soul, never thinking someone could be lying to me, never realizing I was also a dishonest man and a prodigal mark for a con.

In those few moments of truth, I learned that people lie, including me. I learned that trust is not handed out to strangers, but something that is earned. The issue and the learning curve for me, however, are not about squandering money, for we all have done that. But if we're concerned about the money we've squandered and that's the focus, we can remain foolish and greedy. We must move away from the money and consider the foolishness, greed, and dishonesty.

There is so much of the younger brother in me. I am the young prodigal. By the grace of God, I lived through reckless antics in high school, college, and my twenties. By the grace of God and the prayers of my parents and in-laws, God blessed me with a responsible, caring wife who stood by me in the garage that day I was conned. She no doubt spoke her mind, but she has walked beside me as we have both learned the way of wisdom and not foolishness. We have learned that smart people can make foolish mistakes, and it is because we become foolish by our sinful hearts of dishonesty, greed, and pride.

Squandering is not something we want to think about. We want to move on, forget it. Yet there's something cathartic about assessing our squandering. And there is something preventative about it, too. Have you gone to a far country and squandered the good gifts you've been given? This is not an attempt to equivocate all squandering. Some squandering harms people worse than others. Even so, the type and amount of squandering may be less of an issue than the way we respond when we realize what we've done.

Many of us carry embarrassment, at best, or guilt and deep shame, at worst, that can impact how we function, how we view ourselves and others, and how we live in the world. Our squandering has a way of cropping up in our minds regularly. Time we squandered in an abusive relationship. Money we squandered in a business opportunity that went south. Goodwill squandered with a careless word. Peace of mind squandered because of an unwise decision. Health squandered abusing food, drugs, or alcohol.

I choose, through the confession of my squandering, to no longer visit the International Bank of Guilt and Shame (IBGS) but to visit the First National Bank of Squandered Gifts, doing business as "Bank of Wisdom," to see what I can learn from the experiences of squandering that pay dividends today.

Prodigal Prayer

I've thought, spoken, and acted foolishly. I have tried to please people, and it turns out I cannot bring people happiness, even if I try. I want to be the good guy, respected, thought generous, smart, and compassionate but also strong on the important issues, not a pushover but also likable. All this is a fraud when I am interested in this likability more than what is good, true, and just.

6

Need

After he had spent everything, there was a severe famine in that whole country, and he began to be in need.

Ugandan friends told me to put only half of a peri peri pepper on my food, or I would cough and be in pain. We lived in Uganda for seven years with wonderful people, climate, and surroundings. We loved being with Ugandans, eating their homegrown foods like sweet potatoes, peanut sauce, eggplant, and, of course, fried ants.

Peri peri is a dang hot pepper the size of the little button on the side of your phone. So small is this pepper that I quadrupled the Ugandan host's assessment of my wimpy ability to endure peppers. I put two teensy-weensy peppers on my food. I dove in and wondered what all the fuss was about. After the first swallow of food and peri peri, it felt like someone punched me in the neck. My esophagus caught fire. Water down the gullet had the same effect as throwing it on a grease fire. A coughing conniption ensued—*just* as they had predicted. Tears streamed, snot flowed, sweat poured. They'd told me, and I didn't listen.

"Do—*cough!*—people—*two coughs!*—die—*three coughs!*—of peppers?" Meanwhile, half the village blew a gasket laughing at me. They were holding each other up so they wouldn't fall over from hysterics. I was hearing that slow motion background laughing from television shows. "Can permanent damage be done to taste buds?" A compassionate soul brought milk to cool my flaming lips. I had passed the point of soothing dairy—this was a three-alarm blaze. Would I be able to taste chocolate chip ice cream again? These weren't ghost peppers. They were tiny volcanic monsters. I needed the fire department. I don't remember when I stopped hurting, but I made it home, and several days later I tasted again.

A year after the peri peri incident, in 1997, my Ugandan friends were no longer laughing as much. An extreme drought had hit the region, and mothers, like my friend Cathy Waako, wondered aloud how they would feed their children. "There is no rain, no crops, no money, and no food to feed the children," Cathy said. I felt sick for my friend and thousands of vulnerable people in the region east of the Nile River where we served as missionaries. Hunger pains of our friends were compounded by their inability to feed guests, a deeply held value of hospitality and the practice of feeding everyone something when they visited, even if it's peri peri.

Cathy and her husband, Wilson, and their local church organized to distribute food that would be brought from the nearest town. One-hundred-pound bags of corn flour and rice were transported in our pickups and rented trucks to rural points where our friends shared with their neighbors who were suffering. Friends near the Uganda and Kenya border cut cassava from their gardens and shared disease-resistant plants with people a hundred miles away.

Cathy and Wilson had a baby named Louisa, named by an American visitor we had brought to their village. A few months later, I visited a rural hospital where the Waako family had brought Louisa. Cathy, her eyes swollen from weeping, greeted me through quiet sobs and told me the terrible news that Louisa had died. When I asked where the baby was, Cathy pointed to a duffel bag.

The bag was zipped up. *Not in there!* I thought. My heart sank.

Dumbstruck, I couldn't think of anything to say. The thought of the baby in that duffel bag made tears leap from my eyes. But there was no other way for their family to carry the tiny body. To put the body in the dark, hot morgue of the run-down hospital would take money this poor farming family didn't have.

Before I arrived, they were planning to take Louisa's body in the duffel bag on the bus back home. They'd hidden the baby from view because transporting a dead body, no matter how large or small, was an extra charge. People did not want to ride on a bus with a dead body. I drove the Waako family, Louisa bundled up in Cathy's arms, home in my car. Jill's Aunt Mary and Uncle Donny were visiting from the United States and were with us on this visit. Though Mary and Donny did not know the language, they loved Cathy and Wilson with hugs and by shedding tears of parental sorrow with them.

When we arrived at the Waako's home, neighbors gathered to mourn and help the Waako family build a tiny wooden coffin. In the hours that followed, family and friends brought food, firewood, and water to host the mourners. A grave was dug, prayers were said, and Louisa's body was buried.

There has been loose talk among some who go on mission trips to places like Uganda suggesting that a high mortality rate leads Ugandans to have more babies because they know they may lose one or more children. I do not know if that is true at all. But I do know that the pain of losing a child is not any less for someone who has had many children than someone who has had fewer. Nor is the pain any less for someone already living in harsh life conditions. I learned that day that no matter where you live in the world, the grief of losing a child is the grief of losing a child is the grief of losing a child.

In the parable Jesus told, the parents of the younger son had lost their "baby" in a way that also brings pain. The younger son had left home, traveled to a far country, and foolishly spent his inheritance. A famine broke out in that far country, and he began to be in need.

He began to be in need.

Never in my life before that drought in 1997 had I experienced so acutely both externally and internally what it meant to be "in need." Due to food shortages, I could see need on the faces of hungry children and their mothers and fathers. I could feel hunger because we were fasting together. I lost forty pounds the year of the drought. (Years later, I found those pounds.)

I was in need in many other ways, including the need to communicate in another language and culture. One time in a rural church setting, I wanted to say that everyone is part of the family of God. I knew very well how to say the word for God, but I mispronounced the Lusoga word for family. What I said in Lusoga, translated for you back into English, was this: "I warmly invite you into the butt of God."

I thought I was inviting people to something wonderful and did not realize I'd laid such a goose egg. I watched for their reactions. People murmured with restrained smiles, like they might pop. *Good*—I figured I'd struck a chord. I said "butt of God" again, changing it up to an urging.

"Get in the butt of God, folks! Don't wait. All of us belong there."

In church gatherings, women sit with their babies and children on mats, men on wooden benches. After what I said, the women and children were in a better position to pound the floor and have a cleansing belly laugh.

After the first few swells of laughter subsided, another wave would come upon an individual and everyone would start again. The same people who had busted a gasket with me dying of peri peri had yet another reason at my expense to laugh their butts off.

Cathy and her neighbors knew I needed a gift of language, and if it were not for the entertainment value of my verbal gaffes, they might have prayed for me to speak more accurately. My Ugandan friends did pray for me, loved my family, and gave more generously than I'd ever imagined in my life. Other than the months of food shortages, every time I visited the Waako family, relatives and neighbors always sent food home to Jill and the kids. I took home chickens, a turkey, a goat, fried grasshoppers, peanuts, mangoes, oranges, papaya, cassava root, sweet potatoes, bananas—I think the only food they *didn't* send me home with was a cow.

I perceived my Ugandan friends to be in need, but they lived happy lives with most everything they needed. How could I take these things from them? I mean, seriously, how could I take home a goat? If you ever see me personally after reading this book, ask me how I got the goat home, about Kibogroup.org goat project, or about how Jill got a neighbor kid's goat. I have too many goat stories to fit here.

Together, we began to be in need.

When my father was on an operating table eight thousand miles away, I told Wilson and Cathy, and the whole church prayed for my father. They prayed for me, realizing I was homesick and attempting mission work that was over my head. They might have prayed for a missionary with an altogether different tongue, able to hold his peri peri and able to form the words they spoke, but they got stuck with a man in need.

He began to be in need.

Had I squandered support of my family and church in coming so far yet coming up a few feet short? Was I really communicating anything remotely like the gospel of God's love, or about God's backside? Was the answer to get better and stop being in need, or to learn what happens when admitting my need? I did get better at language, but I also got better at confessing my sins, weaknesses, and needs to my Ugandan sisters and brothers.

He began to be in need.

We had come to Uganda with a group of college friends who wanted to "do something bigger than ourselves." Gracious friends, families, and churches supported us to live in Uganda. They sent us to share what we knew about Jesus and how following him can change lives. We were young and facing human needs and problems unlike anything we had seen before. In many ways, we did not have a choice but to be overwhelmed and admit how much we needed. Our supporters also knew how much we remained in need financially, emotionally, spiritually, and in wisdom and skills to be good missionaries.

We began to be in need.

What happened as we learned to admit our needs and our inability to solve all the needs of our Ugandan neighbors? By turns and sometimes all at once, we experienced an AIDS epidemic, bouts of malaria, cholera, the threat of nearby Ebola, border wars with rebel groups in northern Uganda, and violence between ethnic groups. Meanwhile, we tried to hold ourselves together as individuals, families, and a mission team, experiencing our own personal needs. We worked through conflicts with coworkers, weathered illnesses, robberies, car wrecks, and many deaths.

We began to be in need with our Ugandan friends.

Our needs and stories, however, are not the story of life in Uganda. The story is about Cathy and Wilson and thousands of Ugandan friends like the Waako family who confessed their sins, declared their love of Jesus, and decided to live "in need" of this love the rest of their lives. The Waako family and neighbors taught me to look deeper than the younger son's stupidity. There was also a famine in the land. They know that no matter what you do, you are in need. You are not in control as much as you think you are. Need is pervasive. People around you are in need. I am in need. You are in need. Sure, the younger son had made bad choices, but what left him helpless in the end was the famine.

He began to be in need.

7

Pigs

So he went and hired himself out to a citizen of that country, who sent him to his fields to feed pigs. He longed to fill his stomach with the pods that the pigs were eating, but no one gave him anything.

My daughter Anna is a registered nurse who began her career at the same time the coronavirus pandemic started. One day Anna called after a grueling twelve-hour shift and told us three people had died that night on her COVID unit. Along with Anna, other family members, including Toby, Sidney, Hannah, and Gina, have worked directly with coronavirus patients. I have never heard such a deep level of exasperation and desperation in their voices as during the deadliest periods of the global pandemic. I have the deepest respect for my daughter's work as a nurse during the COVID-19 pandemic. I am grateful to her and my other family members and friends working in the medical community.

In the first two years of the global pandemic, there were a half-billion cases of COVID-19 and 14.9 million deaths as a result of the pandemic.[1] Regardless of what you and I think about the pandemic, the sheer number of deaths and amount of grief has changed the world profoundly. How can anyone in the world be unaffected by the pandemic? The ways we work, play, worship, and otherwise interact have changed in big and small ways. We will "get back to normal," but normal will be different in some ways after what the world has collectively been through.

In the middle of the pandemic, I saw a woman's T-shirt that read, "When all this is over, I'll still want you to stay six feet away." Epochs that involve intense events like a pandemic expose corresponding levels of human ingenuity, grief, foolishness, resilience, and witty T-shirts.

Like the pandemic exposing various levels of humanity, a famine exposed the younger son's foolishness and resilience. By foolishness and famine, the younger son had come to the end of his father's wealth. The word coming out of the pandemic was "resilience." The younger son shows resilience when he hires himself out. He takes one of the least desirable jobs imaginable. Far from home, he is a determined and resilient immigrant willing now to be a caretaker of pigs.

If you are a hog farmer or butcher, you already know that some people do not fully appreciate your work. Jesus wasn't exactly a friend to pigs either. One time he sent evil spirits into a herd of hogs and they went careening off a cliff. As an observant Jew, Jesus would not have eaten pork. Because of purity laws and health reasons, pork has been avoided by a huge population of the world, both in the times Jesus lived and today. So when some hear this episode in the parable, they may raise an eyebrow at the younger son in contact with pigs.

Amy-Jill Levine says the younger son's problem, however, is not purity laws and pigs. His problem is that he is hungry.[2] He would gladly have filled himself with the pods the pigs were eating. The disgusting things I've eaten were not preceded by desperate hunger but by dares. The younger son, however, was so hungry that religious rules and bodily disgust would be overcome by a desire for pig slop. Why? Presumably this was the younger son's first job outside of his father's farm. He was an immigrant making anywhere from less than a living wage to no wages at all. This "citizen of that country" gave nothing but the prospect of dining with pigs.

We do not know what the citizen of that faraway country was going through, but we can presume he was also living in famine. He sent this young immigrant to the fields to tend the pigs. No one gave the son a meal, and he got jealous of pigs eating what pigs themselves hesitated to eat: pods from a tree. If pigs had craved tree pods, maybe the Creator would have made them able to stand on their back legs.

Mary Beth Rogers, author of *Cold Anger*, tells a story of Ernie Cortes, an activist and evangelist of good news for poor and oppressed people. Cortes worked alongside people like the younger son who long for something better than the slop their society is offering to people on their side of town. Few people I have met are looking for a handout, yet some churches operate handout programs that steal the dignity of poor people.

What can we do to not steal dignity from people in need? Cortes says we can practice the "Iron Rule." The Iron Rule states, "Never do for people what they can do for themselves."[3] For example, in one church I served at, we welcomed homeless people into our kitchen to eat with us, and we invited them to wash dishes and clean up with us. This is one small way we can preserve the dignity of people who usually want to pitch in and help themselves.

The Iron Rule is an inspirational idea to me—the negative space around the Golden Rule that we don't often discuss or practice. The Golden Rule, known across religions, is a variation of "do unto others as you wish to be done to you." The Iron Rule as an addendum in language parallel to the Golden Rule is this: "Do not do for others what they can do for themselves." A reversed and personalized way of saying this is, "Do not expect for others to do what you can do for yourself."

This points to another small way to honor people with dignity and worth, which is to not rush to financial or charitable assistance. Instead, you can join in prayer and wonder together how a person may solve their own problems with the wisdom they have. One day a few years ago, two women visited our church asking for prayer and financial assistance. As I prayed with the two women, tears streamed down their faces. The Holy Spirit was reminding me in that prayer how these women are beloved daughters of the Most High God. They were struggling to know how much they each were loved. One of the women said she had never heard a prayer like that before, but she would never forget it. Some people do not know they have the capacity to be good or valued. They are living in a faraway country and need to remember the voice of a loving Creator calling them home.

How do parents live the Iron Rule? When you are the parent with a starving child, you care about nothing but how to feed your child. On the other hand, the Iron Rule may become a practice for parents of prodigals who wash, rinse, and repeat the prodigal story. There is a mix of emotions for parents of a prodigal wanderer.

Fort Worth–based preacher Rick Atchley knows what it is like to wonder if your son or daughter is out there starving. Atchley said in a sermon, "I am the father of a rebel" and waiting for a prodigal to come home is heavy. He said your mind wanders to your child. Where is he? You wake up in the middle of the night, and the first thought is of your child. Atchley says he would not wish the pain on anybody. The message of Jesus in this parable has become more tangible to him through the experience of waiting for a prodigal to come home.

Atchley reminds churches that every Sunday, someone's prodigal walks into our churches. Will you welcome these prodigals? Those unseen parents have been praying someone will welcome and embrace their lonely, cynical, or spiritually seeking loved one.

Whether you are praying for a child to come home or praying for a child serving in a historic pandemic, there is a hunger parents feel for children who are far away. Do daughters and sons feel their parents praying from far away? After what the world has been through in the first years of the 2020s, many suffering people have an empty chair at the table, hungry bellies because of wars and famines, and aching souls for prodigals to come home.

Prodigal Prayer

Religious people stayed aloof from Jesus and prodigals and judged them both. Religious people today still try to help the Shepherd separate sheep and goats. The Spirit of Christ does not need our help with sorting sinners and saints. We have been invited instead to love fellow prodigals and find home together.

Help us, Lord, not to stand aloof and sort but to love fellow prodigals and find home together.

8

Sense

When he came to his senses, he said, "How many of my father's hired servants have food to spare, and here I am starving to death!"

In the seventies, a young man named Keith Green was a piano prodigy with a voice and the energy to be a teen idol. He caught the attention of a record company, but the executives decided instead to bank on a little-known guy named Donny Osmond.

Okay, if you are back from the Internet looking up the Osmonds, can we please get back to Keith Green? At fifteen years old, Keith left home to "find himself." In his late teens and early twenties, he played music in a Los Angeles club called the "Blah Blah." He experimented with drugs and world religions. He moved in with a young woman named Melody. One day Keith self-righteously threw away some of Melody's astrology and new age books he did not like. Reminds me of the story I told you about when I self-righteously stole and threw away a poster that did not belong to me.

The couple was on the verge of breaking up when a friend dared them to visit a home Bible study. Keith and Melody were wary of Christians, churches, and people "tripping on them about believing the whole Bible," parts of which Keith believed were not inspired. Keith particularly did not want to join any Jesus freaks ramming the gospel down his throat.

The Bible study was led by eventual founders of the Vineyard churches in California. Melody soon gave her life to Jesus. More time passed and Melody and Keith got married. Around this time, Keith wrote in his journal, "Jesus, you are hereby officially welcomed into me. Now, only action will reveal your effect on me."

Keith started telling his friends how to live, quoting scriptures, giving them Bibles to read. Some friends would have told Keith where he could put the Bible if they had not wanted it for smoking papers. Others were moved by how Keith and Melody lived the love of Jesus. At one time they had more than a dozen people crashing in their home. They shared food and money, and everyone played guitar. Of course they played guitar; it was the seventies. They rented more houses on their street to host homeless and vulnerable people. I do not really know, but I could speculate that those houses may have come open when neighbors saw the street turning into a hippie commune!

Meanwhile, Keith was trying to start his pop music career, but he was rejected by label after record label. He finally gave in and made Christian music. His first two Christian albums were hits and concerts were packed. He scolded audiences for clapping for him and not God. Then Keith pitched the idea of giving away his records "for whatever you can afford." The record company rolled their eyes. The label freed up Keith so he could give his idea a try, on his own. Keith and Melody began their own company and gave away records and tapes.

I was on the receiving end of Keith's ingenious plan to give away music. My sister, Debbie, gave me a Keith Green album. She paid for it. I know I did not. I really do owe Debbie for introducing me to the music of Keith and Melody Green.

The songs were about God's love breaking through, about the mission of Jesus to take the gospel to the world. "Jesus commands us to go," Keith sang. "It should be the exception if we stay." That line, written by both Keith and Melody Green, broke my heart and motivated Jill and me to commit to living seven years in Uganda with a church-planting team mission. This call to go into the world touched both of my sisters, Debbie and Terri, who also served as missionaries in African countries.[1] Love had broken through, and Jill and I also wanted to share the love of God with others.

The younger son in the parable also had a breakthrough. Some English translations say the younger son "came to himself." This is not the first time the writer, Luke, gives internal thoughts of characters who are near Jesus. Between Luke chapters seven and eighteen, more than half a dozen characters have internal, brutally honest thoughts that stop short of repentance.

The first is Simon the Pharisee. He has grave doubts about Jesus, and when he sees a "sinful woman" anointing him, Simon has a full-on conversation with himself about how Jesus can't be a good person because he allows such a sinner to touch his body.

Another teacher of the law is deeply concerned with appearances and wants to cover all his bases as an exceptional rule keeper. As he talks to Jesus, he can't quite keep it all in, so he famously justifies himself by asking, "And who is my neighbor?"

A rich fool from one of Jesus's stories believes he will live forever. He starts talking to himself about building bigger barns to hold all his stuff. He will eat, drink, and be merry. That is, until the man dies. He would not be needing those bonus barns.

Jesus tells another short parable with themes similar to his two-sons story. This parable is about two people who went to the temple to pray: a religious leader called a Pharisee and a tax collector.

> The Pharisee stood by himself and prayed: "God, I thank you that I am not like other people—robbers, evildoers, adulterers—or even like this tax collector. I fast twice a week and give a tenth of all I get."
>
> But the tax collector stood at a distance. He would not even look up to heaven, but beat his breast and said, "God, have mercy on me, a sinner."

Jesus concluded the parable saying, "I tell you that this man, rather than the other, went home justified before God. For all those who exalt themselves will be humbled, and those who humble themselves will be exalted" (Luke 18:10–14). Jesus opposed people who were confident in their own righteousness and who looked down on everyone else.

So the younger son is one of many whose internal thoughts are revealed in Luke's Gospel. Sometimes it takes a crisis to lift our heads and come to our senses. The younger son's hunger and devastation turned his thoughts toward home and "he came to himself." His internal thoughts were, *How many of my father's hired hands have bread enough and to spare, but here I am dying of hunger!*

This ironic realization that his father's hired hands had food while he starved is not necessarily confession. As Philip Yancey says in *Soul Survivor*, "Jesus does not dwell on the prodigal's motive for return. The younger son feels no sudden remorse nor burst of love for the father he insulted. Rather, he tires of a life of squalor and returns out of selfish motives. Apparently, it matters little to God whether we approach him out of desperation or out of longing."[2]

The Greens lived on the edges of desperation and longing for the sake of sharing God's love with others. In the summer of 1982, Keith Green boarded a twin-engine plane with two of his young children and nine others including the pilot. The plane took off from an airstrip nearby their ministry property, but the overloaded plane struggled to gain altitude and clear the trees ahead. The plane crashed shortly after takeoff, less than a mile from the airstrip. Melody and others on the ministry property ran through the woods to get to the burning wreckage. All twelve souls perished. The tragedy left Melody, already pregnant with a fourth child, and a one-year-old, to grieve the loss of Keith and two children.

Not long before the tragedy, Keith had recorded a song about the younger son in the parable. The song was to be part of a full rock opera on stories and parables of Jesus. The project was left incomplete. The most notable incompletion is that the song did not include the story of the elder brother's response to the younger brother returning home.

The song Melody Green produced for her husband posthumously is titled "The Prodigal Son Suite." The song itself became a rock opera to me. I listened to the song over and over in my dorm room and car. I wiped tears waiting for the tape to rewind. It was the first time I had heard a Bible story so beautifully sung.

I do not know if I was crying because I was far from home or because the music and tragedy of the Greens' lives moved me or because my heart was changing. God has seen mixed motives before and is able to sort through them. As Keith wrote in his journal, only action would reveal the effect of this story on me.

Tears may signal that your heart is melting from the icy way you have felt toward others or God. If you are not a crier, a logical decision may need to be made. Hunger, a song while you are far from home, the voice of a loved one, and a teaching of Jesus can all prompt your heart and mind to return to a place of love called home.

Does your heart long for home?

Prodigal Prayer

Brennan Manning prays in *The Ragamuffin Gospel*:

Lord Jesus, we are silly sheep who have dared to stand before You and try to bribe You with our preposterous portfolios. Suddenly we have come to our senses. We are sorry and ask You to forgive us. Give us the grace to admit we are ragamuffins, to embrace our brokenness, to celebrate Your mercy when we are at our weakest, to rely on Your mercy no matter what we may do. Dear Jesus, gift us to stop grandstanding and trying to get attention, to do the truth quietly without display, to let the dishonesties in our lives fade away, to accept our limitations, to cling to the gospel of grace, and to delight in Your love. Amen.[3]

9

Rise

I will set out and go back to my father . . .

In the novel *In My Father's House* by Earnest Gaines, a son returns home to reckon with his father who had abandoned the son and his son's mother. The father had become a pastor with a new wife and children.

Seeing his father for the first time in twenty years, the son admits, "My soul is sick." The son had come to reveal his soul, but his father does not reciprocate. The pastor was preoccupied with his new wife and children, church, and civil rights struggle in a 1960s small town in Louisiana. The son's return and confession jolt the father, who takes his own trip back to his nearby hometown. He confides to an old friend, "I am at war with my soul." Rather than bare his soul to his son and tell him how racism had ripped his life apart, he instead confides in an old friend. The father himself is a prodigal.

Seething with anger, the son had come to town to kill his father. But when he encountered a man with no remorse, calloused through and through, the son's feelings became too much to bear. Facing this chasm between parent and child that he could not traverse, tragically, the son takes his own life.

Home for some people may not be what psychologist John Bowlby calls a "secure base," a safe place of retreat from the world. What would it feel like to not have a secure base of return, to be a son who was not returning to that secure base but to take the life of his own father? What would it be like to have a parent in prison? What would it be like to not have a mother or father, to be an orphan? You may not have to imagine because you know intimately these feelings of abandonment or distance. Where is that secure base of return that allows the daughter to say, "I will return to my mother"?

The son in the story of Jesus widens the gap as far as possible, to the point of desperation and starvation. The son's organs are shrunken; he is emaciated and constantly chilled. He is listless and his soul is sick, but he remembers his father. He has come to his senses and remembers how his father provides for his workers in contrast to his hunger pains. Even in the fog of deprivation from starvation, the son has one clear thought: "I will rise up and go to my father."

When he rises, he does not know if the father will receive him. In fact, he has already hedged his bet and will offer to work for the father and live with the servants. He wonders if his father will even accept him back as a servant, not to mention as a family member.

Some people have a home base but do not want to return there. Is this how you feel right now about home? Maybe home for you is not a secure base but a stressful or distant place. For many who have experienced physical or emotional abuse, understandably, home is not a helpful place or healing metaphor. If this is how you feel about home, this parable can help reshape your ideas about home to be larger than each of our own experiences alone.

I have parents who never left my childhood hometown, who still worship at the church where I grew up. I have for all my life been able to return to the place of my birth and find family there. I can visit my siblings, my mother, and my in-laws and be welcomed and share mutual love. Not everyone has this. Have you ever acknowledged the secure base of return you have or do not have and how it might be affecting you?

Moving far from home and facing challenges of work, hunger, and loneliness are a strong elixir that turn our faces toward home. Away from home, we can almost smell our mother's cooking and taste her unconditional love. Away from home, we may fondly remember how much we love dad jokes, no matter how much we groaned when he told them.

As a father with adult children further away now, I realize how much I miss the loving presence, wisdom, and humor of my children. Having been raised by a teacher and preacher, our children have taught and preached and inspired us as much as we have them. Jill and I are blessed that they stay in touch and want to visit home and want us to visit them. We know this is not the case for everyone and pray you will find ways to close the chasm. We too may have some canyons in the future that we will have to cross to return to one another.

Some good news for those in the middle of tension between mother and daughter is that these relationships can blossom later in life. The good news for the father whose teenage son is not talking to you now is that someday he will text you and ask what you think about the war in Ukraine or the price of a car. What dad doesn't love getting a text from his daughter asking, "Hey Dad, how much should a brake job cost?"

My sole ab workout during the pandemic was laughing at an insurance company's commercials about becoming your parents. The humor of this idea opens us up for the punch in the gut when we realize we are making some of the same mistakes as our parents or grandparents. We also carry forward some good or neutral qualities. We can't help it. Like it or not, we become something like our parents in good, bad, or neutral ways.

I found myself texting my daughter on her spring break trip to see how she was doing and where she was on her vacation. That's like my dad. Dad used to call when I was traveling. He enjoyed visualizing where we were, vicariously traveling with us. In his final days of life, he sang his best Willie Nelson, "On the Road Again" as we pushed his wheelchair. For those who feel more distant from loved ones than a spring break trip, this desire to connect may grow strong enough that a radical action is needed. Some of us need to get up and return or go and find a loved one.

I believe God has placed many secure bases of return that may not be your family. My brother Toby, my sister-in-law Debbie, and my sister Terri have all very specifically extended the prodigal base of return beyond family members. They, like my parents, have always hosted and housed prodigals like no others I have known.

What would it be like for a parent to reveal their heart to a child who returns? My parents have long revealed their mistakes, faults, sins, and regrets, and this has been a healing balm to me. No matter what the relationship with parents, no matter what race, ethnicity, or place in life you are in, there is a way to rise up and look for a secure base of return. In the novel by Gaines, the son rises up and returns to his father to kill him. By being present earlier in his life, the father may have prevented twenty years of pain in the son's life. Even when the son returns, the father is still distant, and another tragedy occurs. What if the father had admitted his own brokenness and prodigal sins against the son and the son's mother? Rather than death, could the son have found healing in the father's revelation?

Not everyone can rise up and go to their father or mother. Some of us, like the characters in the novel, put distance between ourselves and family members, and the results can be tragic. Not everyone can do what the younger son in the parable does. Even so, the son did not know how his family would receive him. He took a great risk by returning home. The image of going home or of a parent receiving you home may not feel healing or soothing to you. It is important to name this and be aware in your soul how you feel.

What risks must you take to return to a secure base you may call home?

Prodigal Prayer

The younger brother's words, "I will go to my Father," inspired the church father John Chrysostom to say: "let us draw nigh to God. . . . it is we who put ourselves far off: for 'I am a God' we read 'at hand and not a God afar off.'"[1]

Father, as I pray, I realize you are near to me, even if I act like you are far away. Help me to return to you, for I have moved myself far away.

10

Sin

I will . . . say to him: Father, I have sinned against heaven and against you.

Early one morning, I sat down at an airport bar, hoping they were serving coffee. A few minutes later, a man walked up and slammed his bag down, angry that the bar was not serving alcohol in the morning. Did he need a drink to settle his nerves for his upcoming flight? Who knows. I had work to do. I was waiting for coffee—my addiction to settle my nerves.

I had a Bible, pen, and notebook on the bar, reviewing a sermon. Time passed and the man—I'll call him Sam—asked if that was a Bible I was reading. He knew that onion-skin-rattling sound. He said his grandfather was a preacher. His father was a preacher. Him? No, he'd really made a mess of his life. I wanted to say, "Preachers are pretty good at that, too," but I refrained.

"We all make messes of our lives," I said. This was no revelation to either of us.

I said a silent prayer. *God, I'm available. If you want me to say something now, Holy Spirit, show me what to say.*

Then I said, "How does it feel when you disappoint your father?"

At the mention of disappointing his father, tears instantly welled up in Sam's eyes.

"I go to church, but I can't stop drinking," Sam said.

"Does your church have a substance abuse recovery program?"

"Yes, but I've never been."

Tears were streaming down the man's face now. Was he still upset about not having a drink yet? Had the Holy Spirit helped me with a few good words that landed on his heart? Sam wiped his eyes with a bar napkin. The bartender opened the bar and asked Sam what he wanted.

"Nothing," Sam said.

"You know what, Sam? God is closer to you now than the blood in your veins." Sam said he'd never heard that before. If the Holy Spirit gave me that word, it was a long time ago through a trusted friend and mentor named Terry Smith.

We shook hands and parted. It was the end of a long business trip for Sam, and he was heading home.

After the younger son decides to get up and return to his father, he rehearses a three-part speech. The first thing he wants to say to his father is, "I have sinned against heaven and against you."

Amy-Jill Levine wonders if the younger son really repented. Was the younger son contrite, or just hungry? Levine thinks first-century hearers would have heard not contrition but conniving. The son recalls that his dad has food, shelter, and work. Unlike the lamb and the coin, the son is yet unfound. He has only found his senses, which leads him to food. Levine says, "He recovers his true nature—he is described as 'coming to himself'—and that self is one who knows that daddy will do anything he asks."

Levine reminds us of how similar the young son sounds to the "sorry, not sorry" pharaoh of Egypt who said to Moses and Aaron, "I have sinned against the Lord your God, and against you." The youngest son is mouthing the same words as the Egyptian pharaoh? Israel is also not above insincerity. Levine quotes a rabbinic commentary *Leviticus Rabbah*: "When Israelites are reduced to eating carob pods, they repent."[1] Levine concludes the son is no more repentant than the pharaoh. David Buttrick's thought bubble for the younger son is, *I'll go to my Daddy and sound religious.*

I could go on about the younger son's insincerity, but I must consider my own insincerity and sin. I'm learning to ask myself questions beneath the hunger and discover motivations for my religious speeches. What emotion is my gluttony feeding and covering? Why do I want to please people when it's clear I can't? Why do I have this envy of other people's success and how is it affecting what I do? Why do I feel like an imposter? How am I going to fend off these lustful thoughts and remain faithful to my wife, my children, and to God? Why do I feel lazy and lack interest in the Bible right now? Why am I in debt and what does that say about my life? Why do I care about others seeing me serving or giving? Why is this thing upsetting me and how do I learn to let go?

I like the radical reframing a Christian counselor named Terry Ewing helped me accept about myself. I am a stick man—another word for prodigal. Though popular American Christianity pumps up the idea that I must be a strongman in the strong armor of God, I am not a strongman inside strong armor. I am a stick man inside the strong armor of God. I am not saved by a strong family line, denomination, actions, works, culture, service, baptism, or the number of sermons I preach, books I write, good deeds I perform, nice words I say, or anything else.

I am saved by grace through faith in Christ who loves me and gave himself for me, who became a human on the world's behalf.

Like the younger son rehearsing speeches, I am a hypocrite who knows I will sin again. I need the continual washing and forgiveness of God in Christ by the power of the Holy Spirit. I am a faithful, struggling, striving, growing, fallible, messed up human being redeemed by Jesus Christ.

I do not know why Sam listened to me that day in the airport. It was too early. I did not want to talk. I had a no-caffeine headache. I had a sermon to prepare, and here's this guy asking me if that is a Bible? He knew it was. Was he a prodigal turning his face toward home?

I wonder if what Sam said to me was a dress rehearsal for what he wanted to say to his dad. Sam was in the very place of the younger son, rehearsing his speech, testing on a barstool what he would later say at his father's table. I wonder if he reached out to say, "Father, I have sinned against heaven and against you."

So many of us stay in rehearsal, having something to say but never saying it, never repenting, never saying I'm sorry. When prolonged feelings of cynicism, anger, or compassion fatigue set in, I seek out counsel from close family, friends, mentors, and professional counselors. I have entrusted my heart to skilled counselors many times in my prodigal life. When I can feel my heart hardening toward others, toward God, I turn like the youngest son and say, "Jesus Christ, son of God, have mercy on me a sinner."

Prodigal Prayer

The Book of Common Prayer invites the church to say with the prodigal son, *"I will arise and go to my father, and I will say to him, 'Father, I have sinned against heaven and before you; I am no longer worthy to be called your son.'"*[2]

11

Worthy

"I am no longer worthy to be called your son."

"I have to trust God." That is what Renee would say no matter how abysmal things got on the streets of Denver, Colorado, where she lived for many years. When Robbie Goldman and the Dry Bones Denver staff met Renee, she had become homeless as a teenager. For Renee, being homeless felt safer than the home in which she had grown up. For homeless youth on the streets of Denver, home is a four-letter word. Home is a place of abuse. Home is not a stable base where they might safely and happily return.

Renee blamed her mother for many of her problems. Renee had narcolepsy and heart problems that required surgery. She wondered if she would survive and see the other side of homelessness. In her mind, she wanted to think home would supply a safe place of return when she was sick, but it wasn't safe for her yet. Renee remained on the streets, in and out of emergency rooms, and finally got the surgery she needed to repair her heart condition.

Renee celebrated birthdays on the streets and survived to see her twenties. The physical and emotional pain she endured led her into drug addiction. She fought off addiction and continually said, even in her lowest moments, "I have to trust God." She knew she could trust God. She just did not know if she could trust people. She wondered if she could trust life itself. Life came to her anyway, in the form of pregnancy. She had a baby, but because of her living situation, she lost custody of her child. Later she had a second child and again lost custody. She loved her children very much and never gave up her visitation rights. Still, she longed for their daily touch, voices, spirits, and their eyes peering at her and trusting her and reminding her to hope.

When you are on the street and you have so much against you, it takes a dozen daily decisions to move in a positive direction, to get sober, to find a secure place of return each night of your life. She began working at the Purple Door, a coffee roaster in Denver run by friends of Dry Bones.

Dry Bones Denver exists for homeless young people who think they are no longer worthy to have a name like "son" or "daughter." So that image of the Purple Door symbolizes a secure base of protection and love. What touches hearts like Renee's is that Dry Bones staff call her by name and tell her she is royalty; that is the power and the point of purple.

Matt and Nikki Wallace, founders of Dry Bones, gave a copy of Brennan Manning's *The Ragamuffin Gospel: Visual Edition* to a street kid. In the inside front cover they wrote, "You are deeply loved. Dry Bones staff." When the young man received the book, he sat down next to Matt and Nikki and began crying.

A few days later, he told them that he read the book cover to cover. He said he loved the message in the book, but more than that, he loved the inside front cover. He said he had picked up the book every day, opened the front cover, and just stared at the words, "You are deeply loved." He then said, "Matt, I think I believe this." Matt said later, "I desperately want every street kid in Denver to no longer be able to say, 'No one has ever loved me.'"[1]

For Renee, believing she was loved took much longer. Dry Bones walked with Renee for ten years before she started believing what they were saying: that she is deeply loved, even royalty. Renee realized this changes everything, and there were steps she had to take to live into this new identity. She discovered over a period of years that she had to give in and go home to get something back from broken relationships. Her mother's home was safer than the streets. It was a place of stability where she and her mother could now improve their relationship. After moving home, Renee had the secure base to move from prodigal to parent.

Defying odds against her, Renee decided to pursue the return of her children to her lawful and rightful custody as their mother. She fought custody battles, showing up to court dates to plead her case. Renee negotiated relationships with her mother, her children, attorneys, and the state in courts, all the time trying to stay employed. She longed for a decisive victory that would bring her children home. Her first mantra remained, "I have to trust God." Now she had a second mantra: "I have to get my children back."

Finally, after years of fighting for custody, she got her children back at ages four and five. She accessed wraparound support services provided by Dry Bones Denver, the city, and other nonprofits. One of those services included a pediatrician who was on call to help with the children's health.

One night after the children had been living with her again for months, she called 911 because of a medical emergency. Very soon after arriving, a paramedic began questioning Renee's ability as a mother to care for her children. Renee lives with the fear of being labeled a bad mother, even by the very people who are meant to give care. First responders, emergency room nurses, and doctors receive people regularly who they must assess for fitness to care for children who come into the emergency unit. That is part of a medical worker's job.

For Renee's part, she knew her job in this situation was to advocate for herself, her children, and to reach out for help. Renee called her pediatrician, whom she put on speaker phone with the paramedics. The pediatrician affirmed her as a fit mother who cares for her children and then stayed on the speaker phone with Renee to ensure quality care. The doctor called ahead to the hospital, where she received the best possible care for the emergency with her child.

Robbie calls Renee's life a "double prodigal story" because she returned home and then realized she must go as a mother and restore her prodigal children to her care and loving warmth of home.

During my visits to Denver, spending time on the streets with Dry Bones and the people they love and serve, the Goldmans and Wallaces have taught me that "just" statements do not help prodigals. A "just" statement is most often formed as a question we assume on others as an easy step. Why don't you *just* get off drugs? Why don't you *just* get a job? Why don't you *just* go home? These "just" statements are not just or fair. These attempts to help only perpetuate lack of understanding, animosity, disgust, and separation between people. The worst thing of all is that these just statements play into the mind of the prodigal who believes already that she is not worthy.

The younger son in the story of Jesus rehearses a speech he wants to give to his father, and it includes a mantra he now recites to himself: "I am no longer worthy to be called my father's son." This sense of unworthiness is a realization that will be tested when he arrives home. Will his father agree with this self-assessment by the younger son?

Like the younger son, so many are unsure that God loves them. Even for those who have loving parents and a secure base of return, one of the hardest truths to live into is receiving the love and grace God offers as a gift. I have spoken with many people who have never believed they are beloved in the first place. Meanwhile, I've spoken with some Christian people who believe they can only call themselves and other baptized believers in Jesus Christ beloved "children of God." What can we do about this slipping away of our identity as beloved children?

I believe each human being is created by God in the image of God and is thus a child of God. No matter who you are, what you have done, and where you have been, you are a beloved child of God. Some people haven't realized it yet. This realization is so important that some theologians call it life's ultimate goal. Henri Nouwen wrote to a skeptic and said, "Dear friend, being the beloved is the origin and the fulfillment of life in the Spirit of God."[2] That is amazing to me. This fact of God's love for you changes everything.

It changed everything for Renee. For more than a decade, Renee never lost her desire to get back home. Renee kept saying, "I have to get back home. I have to get my kids. I have to trust God." And she did all those things. She is a prodigal, beloved child, and a faithful parent like the God she so faithfully trusts.

In Renee's story, I hear echoes of the fifteenth-century Christian mystic Margery Kempe. Her opponents in England tried constantly to discredit and diminish her love and trust in God. One of Margery's special gifts was that she saw visions, mostly of Jesus but sometimes of biblical people. She was also visited by demons and quoted Scripture against them. Some dismissed her as demon possessed, and like Jesus, many of Margery's own family thought she was insane.

In what is considered the first autobiography in English, Margery wrote about social and domestic issues but mostly about her intimate relationship with Jesus. Throughout her autobiography, *The Book of Margery Kempe*, she writes in the voice of Jesus who says, "I ask you, daughter, to give me nothing but love. You can never please me more than to have me always in your love, and you shall never, in any penance that you can do on earth, please me so much as to love me."[3]

Margery wrote these things over and over because she doubted the truth that God really loved her. I imagine being told you are demon possessed does not help you feel loved. Likewise, the younger son thought he was not worthy to be called his father's son. I have wrestled with my own unworthiness to be a minister of the good news when I know I am a sinner. I learned over many years that taking on the identity of a prodigal who is loved is precisely what is needed to minister the healing love of God to others. Renee very visibly wrestled with being God's beloved. Taking on the identity of a beloved prodigal was the Purple Door to becoming a prodigiously loving parent and teaching her children that they too are beloved of God.

Prodigal Prayer

My pride craves recognition for what I do, or give, or even contribute, whether I'm at church, home, or work. I have lashed out or been passive aggressive toward people who do not give me credit for what I think I do or who I think I am. All that seems so childish, but taking the posture of a little child when I pray seems to actually be a good daily remedy for pride and desire for control. The term that helps me remember this is the word "Abba." It's the affectionate term, similar to "Daddy," that Hebrew children use when they talk with their fathers.

Abba, I want to do everything on my own. And I don't like asking for help. I'm aware of how much I desire for others to think and say good things about me. I want the praise that should more rightly go to you. Remind me that I am your child and that your love for me is enough. I keep forgetting this. Help me remember.

12

Worker

". . . make me like one of your hired servants."

Once there was a teenager who stole from her mother. She ran far away. In that place, she lived on the money she stole from her mother. When the money was all gone, she was reduced to becoming a wandering beggar.

Her mother, meanwhile, continually looked for her daughter but never found her. The mother grew richer, however, far beyond anything the daughter ever knew.

Years passed, and the daughter found her way back to her hometown, where she continued begging. One day she saw an entourage, and she thought it must be a royal person. In her reduced state, the daughter did not recognize that the famous person was her mother.

The mother saw the daughter and recognized her. Pretending she did not recognize the daughter, the mother offered her a modest position in her entourage. The daughter accepted the position and worked hard. Over time, the young woman earned greater responsibility in the wealthy woman's business affairs.

More years passed, and the mother was on her death bed. The woman revealed to her daughter their true relationship. The daughter would become the heir of everything.

This story is an adaptation of a Buddhist story found in the *Lotus Sutra*. The Buddhist version, which Zen teacher James Ford has interpreted, was about a father and son. While there are critical differences between the story found in the Bible and the one found in the *Lotus Sutra*, there are also important similarities.[1]

Both stories offer a path of reconciliation. Both parables are about lost children returning home. Both parables open us to the deep longing for home that is part of what it means to be human. The Buddhist version of the story plays out a line in the story of Jesus: "Treat me like one of your servants." The child is offered a place in the entourage to earn back family trust and pay back something of what was lost.

Many Christians sideline notions of earning love and redemption. Yet, we hide in our hearts secret notions that we must perform to be loved. The younger son in Jesus's parable plans to tell the father, "Treat me like one of your servants." The younger son wants to work and pay back what he owes. The story Jesus tells does not play out any payback. The intention of the younger son, however, is clear. He intends to work under the authority of the father's house as a servant.

I wonder why it pains us to see someone squander wealth and have to start over with nothing, because prodigally wasting wealth is one action Jesus asked followers to do. There is more than one way to be wasteful and prodigal with wealth. Rather than squander it on foolish living, we have the freedom to give it all away, again and again.

Many of us know a romantic mythology about two men separated by hundreds of years. What connects them across centuries and is often overlooked is their true stories. They both prodigally wasted wealth and talent in order to work in dedicated service to the Lord.

The first of these two men was a wealthy Italian in the 1200s. He was attending mass at the Church of the Portiuncula, outside of Assisi, when the text for the day was Matthew 10:7–9:

> As you go, proclaim the good news, "The kingdom of heaven has come near." Cure the sick, raise the dead, cleanse the lepers, cast out demons. You received without payment; give without payment. Take no gold, or silver, or copper in your belts. (NRSVA)

When the young man heard the words of Jesus to his disciples, to go and preach and take no money, he stood up and said, "This is what I wish, this is what I seek, this is what I long to do with all my heart!"

He kicked off his shoes, took off his fancy clothes, and wrapped a rough cloth around himself. His change of clothing symbolized his change of heart, a prodigal come home. Francis of Assisi would go on to preach a message of repentance and love of all humanity and creation.

This story about St. Francis struck a chord with me because a man in my family tree made a similar renunciation of wealth and committed his life to spreading generosity and good news. This second person who squandered wealth and talent to serve God and others is my great uncle five times removed, John Chapman. In the early 1800s, John heard a preacher say to a crowd in a frontier town, "Where is the modern-day John the Baptist, who dresses in camel hide and preaches repentance?!"

Uncle John took up the challenge and found an animal skin pelt to wear. He often gave his shoes away to someone who needed them worse than he did, which left him barefooted. His actions showed his prodigal heart of repentance and submission. The word John the Baptist and Jesus preached was about admitting we are prodigals who need to turn around, be found, and come home to the love of God. This about-face of repentance can be the hardest thing a prodigal will ever do, and the best.

John Chapman also planted apple seeds to grow trees for frontier families. With no refrigeration, apple cider vinegar was needed for pickling produce and hard cider was popular for pickling people. Though there is some legend around his popular name, "Johnny Appleseed," John Chapman was indeed a real person, and my ancestor. There is mythology to his story, but he was truly a believer in God and began many conversations in the frontier with a Bible in his hand and the question, "Care for some fresh news from heaven today?" Years ago, I began asking my ancestor's question to hearers of a sermon or Bible reading. When opening the Bible, I ask, "Care for some good news from heaven today?" Of course, I wait for a response to hear if people are willing to admit we all need some good news today!

The good news from heaven from this part of the parable is that the very idea of working as a hired hand in the father's household can motivate a prodigal to come home. This idea comes to the younger son. It is the last thought he has before turning himself toward home.

Care for some good news from heaven today?

13

Return

So he got up and went to his father.

Ernest Hemingway wrote a short story, titled "The Capital of the World," about a young man named Paco who wants to be a matador. On the way to telling this story of Paco the waiter who wants to be a bullfighter, Hemingway tells a joke from Madrid about how popular the name Paco is. Here is my paraphrase of Hemingway's joke, turned into a short story itself, about how deep our need is to return to homemade love.

There was a father whose son rebelled and left home. The father never stopped searching. Finally, in Madrid, in another desperate attempt to find his son, the father placed an ad in the newspaper. The ad the father placed read, "Dear Paco, meet me in front of the Hotel Montana at noon. All is forgiven. Papa."[1]

The father arrived in the square early and watched the large clock as it approached noon on the day the ad was placed. Would Paco show? The father was trembling in hope of seeing his son.

He feared his son did not see the ad. He feared he did see the ad but rejected the offer.

Close to noon, young men began to appear from all directions and walk toward where Paco's father was standing.

That day in front of the Hotel Montana, eight hundred Pacos showed up.

Each Paco had left home, only to realize how much the love of his father and mother meant to him. Each Paco longed for parental love.

I remember the places I lived in college never really feeling like home until I'd left on a trip and returned. I felt like I was returning to a place of retreat again, almost like home. This leaving and thinking about home, sometimes with prompting like an ad, is often what brings us to our senses and turns us again toward home. G. K. Chesterton said, "There are two ways of getting home; and one of them is to stay there. The other is to walk round the whole world till we come back to the same place; and I tried to trace such a journey in a story I once wrote."[2] Home does not become home until you leave and return. That's what the son had done. He'd left and now his thoughts and face were turning back home.

As he went to his father, what did the younger son hope to receive or accomplish? The son does not say what he wants to receive. We only know that the younger son is hungry and is willing to be his father's servant. The son does not offer to repay the money he has squandered. The father would be within his rights to give the son exactly what he asked for, a place with the hired hands, stripped of his sonship. What will the father do? How will he respond to the son's return?

I love the game of hide and seek. The thrill of someone searching for me and finding me gives me chills still. I'll never forget playing the sardines version of hide and seek with my wife and children. One person hides, and when each person finds the hider, they join in hiding until the last person is searching. When everyone is found, everyone squeals and laughs with glee. The thrill of being found reminds us of the exhilaration of being lost, searched for, and found.

Hide and seek offers another metaphor of turning toward home. When the game is over, someone shouts, "Come out, come out, wherever you are!" James Ford says metaphorically, this phrase about coming out of hiding can be, "Come home, come home, all is forgiven."[3]

Brené Brown's TED talk and first books on the subject of vulnerability and courage are extremely popular because so many of us tend to hide without seeking. Brown's ideas of vulnerability lead us to show up courageously when we do not know or cannot control the outcome. If we do the relational work, we may learn to confess hidden shame in our closest relationships.[4]

This kind of prodigal relationship work is not new. It is part of the ancient way of interacting with the stories of Jesus. North African church father Augustine understood the parable as an allegory and read the corresponding characters as spiritual symbols. For Augustine, the father is God, and Augustine saw himself as the younger son who had left home and was far away. Then difficult circumstances came into his life (symbolized by the famine) that caused him to return to God. It was at this crucial moment that Augustine called upon the Lord, writing in *Confessions*, Book III, "Every vain hope at once became worthless to me; and I longed with an incredibly burning desire for an immortality of wisdom, and began now to arise, that I might return to You." Later, in Book VIII, Augustine wrote to God, "You never depart, and we scarcely return to You."[5]

I wonder if Augustine would have liked Hemingway's little joke about Paco. Much like the story Jesus tells, quotes and stories from Augustine to Hemingway are emotional and singular.

Most often, however, reconciliation and forgiveness happen over extended timelines in complex family situations. Still, there is that simple word to Paco, "all is forgiven," that transcends distance and complexity.

Have you ever had such an offer from a loved one, that all is forgiven? What did it feel like when forgiveness washed over you? Or are you still resisting the offer to meet in front of the Hotel Montana?

Prodigal Prayer

When our children were young, and we read bedtime stories, we would often ask them, "What's the most important thing on earth?" And the children responded, "Knowing God." In those same tender years of my children's lives, I wrote this prayer for them:

Dear God,

You are the great Father of the fathers.

You are the one in whom every father becomes a child.

Teach me how to love and raise my children.

For my children are walking by my side as I walk with you—may they also take your hand.

My deep desire for my children is that they know you, that you will draw them near to your side, and they will come to you, humbly seeking your face.

Give them faith, Father, and lead them when it is time for them to take the plunge of faith, to be baptized with Jesus in the depths.

And all their days on earth, may they find new life in you; and when their days on earth are finished, Father, raise them up!

Until then, you've given me the responsibility to raise them up.

Give me courage to raise them in your love and light.

14

Run

But while he was still a long way off, his father saw him and was filled with compassion for him; he ran to his son . . .

British Olympic four-hundred-meter runner Derek Redmond entered the semifinal heat of the race, determined to move ahead and even medal in the 1992 Barcelona Olympic Games. Because of an injury four years earlier, Redmond had to withdraw from the 1988 games.

Redmond was halfway through the four-hundred-meter semifinal when the worst thing for a runner happened, again. In the middle of the race, he tore a hamstring. On his face was a look of surprise then excruciating pain as the field of runners sailed past him and left him behind.

All runners had completed the race, except Redmond, who hobbled on the far side of the track. When he fell to the surface of the track, medics came to his aid, but Redmond refused treatment.

He rose and pushed on, limping and hopping his way around the last half of the track.

Tens of thousands in the stadium watched in stunned silence with pained expressions as Redmond tried to finish. Suddenly, a man came bounding down one of the aisles and jumped the wall onto the track. What was the man doing? He was not authorized to be on the track, but he was heading toward Redmond. Several security guards tried to stop the man, but he pushed one of the guards aside and kept running toward Redmond.

It was Redmond's father, Jim, and he now reached his son on the track.

"You don't have to do this," Redmond's father told him.

"Yes, I do," Derek told his father.

"Well, then we're going to finish together," Jim said.

Jim Redmond put his arm around his son, Derek, and together they walked toward the finish line. Close enough now, Jim stepped back and allowed Derek to cross the finish line on his own. The crowd of thousands gave the father and son a standing ovation, many wiping tears from their faces. Not only is this one of the greatest Olympic moments of the human spirit, but it is also a beautiful picture of the father who runs to meet the son.

One of the things I love about the sport of running is that everyone has their own form. If you have been running for a long time with a group of people, you can even tell from far away who is running by their gait. While the son was still in the distance but visible from home, the father knew who it was. Sick and weak as the son was, the father still recognizes him. Then the father does something surprising. The father does what is enacted in the other two stories Jesus tells. The father does not wait. The father runs to the son.

A lot of fiction has been preached up about how fathers in biblical times would not run, would have rejected the son who came home. Amy-Jill Levine says a lot of what we assume about the parable comes from asking the wrong people. Levine says preachers like me wanting to know more about what a father might have done in this situation should ask women. Not going to disagree with Levine there! Levine cites biblical scholar Carol Schersten LaHurd, who asked women in Yemen, "What would your husband do if his son returned home after wasting all his money?" The women unanimously agreed that the father would lovingly welcome the son, especially if he were a child of his old age.[1]

The upshot of what Levine and LaHurd are saying is that we often make up stuff about Middle Eastern and Near Eastern cultures and read it back into the parable. The biggest concern Levine has is that we should not liken the very Jewish faith Jesus practiced to a bad father. This Jewish father is often portrayed with arms folded, disowning the son. In contrast, the "Christian father" knows how silly all that is, hikes up his robe, and runs with unbridled joy that people in Israel never knew! Nah, Israel knew God as a pursuing, running God. God has been chasing Israel from the very first stories of Abraham and Sarah. This parable adds an intimate detail to the collective experience of Israel being pursued by God. God has always been and always will be a runner. In Jesus, the pursuit continues. In the power of the Holy Spirit, the pursuit of God has always been for all people, not just the people of Israel.

I wonder what I would have done if my child was hurt and trying to finish an Olympic race like Derek Redmond. Would I push aside the guards, jump the wall, and run to them? There are times when we as parents do not care what anyone thinks. Whatever the costs or consequences, we are running to the side of our children. I ran and entered races with my daughter, Anna, and son, Jacob, from middle school to college. I had torn and repaired knees since high school, so I run in shoes that are super cushioned. It's like running on marshmallows in a dream: you don't really get anywhere, and when you're done, you are just glad it's over. Whether running with Anna or Jacob, we would always run together for a while, but they routinely beat me to the finish line.

Racecourses, volleyball courts, and soccer fields have allowed me to shout, "That's my daughter!" to Ashley and Anna, fulfilling my duty as father to embarrass them. Few things rev up parents like their child playing sports! One day when Jacob was in eighth grade, I was watching as he competed in the Tulsa Run. When I saw the form of Jacob coming up Boston Avenue in downtown Tulsa, he was nine minutes ahead of the pace we had talked about him running that day. I couldn't believe it.

I began running on the sidewalk paralleling Jacob on the racecourse. I was knocking people over and shouting, "Finish strong, Jacob!" When I bumped into people I would shout back to them, "That's my son!" I made it past the barriers and met Jacob coming across the finish line. Jacob had run so hard for more than an hour that he crossed the finish line and fell into my arms. A *Tulsa World* photographer was there and captured the moment. I treasure the image of us finishing together and embracing at the finish line.

The father has sprinted to his son, now panting and catching his breath, no more concerned than Jim Redmond or me about what bystanders thought of this old man's running style. The parable invites us to imagine a loving parent who runs out to meet us wherever we are. Have you fallen on the track? Ready to fall into the arms of love? We can imagine a God who runs with joy alongside us and helps us finish the race.

Prodigal Prayer

Lord, my worth, my identity, is wholly and always determined by you. I am not saved by my family line, culture, race, baptism, gender, denomination, politics, or how many good deeds I perform.

I am saved by grace through faith in Christ who loves me and gave himself for me, who became a human on the world's behalf. I am made sin-free, but I am not perfect in my practices. I will fail daily, and I fully accept that without undue feelings of failure.

15

Kiss

He . . . threw his arms around him and kissed him.

Croatian-born theologian Miroslav Volf spoke at a conference, claiming we should embrace our enemies as God in Christ has embraced us. After the lecture someone asked him, "But can you embrace a četnik?" The četnik were like Nazis to Croatians—Serbian enemies who herded people into concentration camps, raped and brutally murdered them, burned churches, destroyed cities. This was a war in the nineties with horrific genocide like the world has seen too many times in history, and tragically continues in the twenty-first century.

Volf was caught between the demand of his fellow Croatians who were oppressed and seeking justice, and the gift of forgiveness the Crucified Lord offered to the perpetrators. How could he remain loyal to both? To the question, "But can you embrace a četnik?" Volf replied, "No, I cannot—but as a follower of Christ I think I should be able to." His book, *Exclusion and Embrace*, is

Volf's longer response to this haunting question, and he explores the embrace of the father and the son in the story of Jesus.

Could the embrace and kiss be a model for the radical embrace of the ultimate other, the evil oppressor? Volf focuses on two themes of the parable: "the father giving himself to his estranged son and his receiving the son back into his household."

Rather than translate the story into rigid theological allegory, Volf reads the story characters as family members in Jesus's real world. Developing a "theology of embrace," he brings the parable into today's world, the very real and specific civil war in the former Yugoslavia. Too many nations, including the United States, know the heartache and destruction of civil wars and the ongoing social, religious, and political upheaval.

The prodigal son story supplies imagery and depth necessary to expand on the shifting identities of family members who have been ripped apart by a civil war. The son's goal had been to "un-son" himself, to exclude himself from the family—a major breach in intensely communal family systems. Famine, betrayal to foreigners, and hunger are his lot. Only in this experience of "alterity," as Volf calls it, a radical change of circumstances, does the younger son come to his senses. Remembering his father, his memory of sonship, he grasps his only hope of survival. Volf says, "There is no coming to oneself without the memory of belonging."[1]

The son will return with the memory and hope of reestablishing sonship, but the sonship will be different because it has been breached. He will be the son who was not worthy to be called son, one like a hired hand, reconfiguring "obligations and expectations." With this new identity of unworthiness, the younger son sets out for home.

What happens next is a turning point both in the story of the younger son and in theological reflection about how relationships—divine and human—hurt and heal. Frederick Buechner gets a whiff of the lost son a mile away. "Smelling of pig and cheap gin, the prodigal comes home bleary-eyed and dead broke, but his father's so glad to see him anyway that he almost falls on his face," Buechner writes in *Peculiar Treasures*.[2]

No filthy smell deters the father from what he does next. He wrapped his reeking son in his arms and kissed him. The kind of reshaped identities necessary for the father and son to embrace and kiss is the groundbreaking theological work Volf does around this story and the historical realities of our times.

The moment of embrace is captured in Rembrandt's famous painting, "Return of the Prodigal Son." I once placed a replica of Rembrandt's painting on the platform with me during a sermon on this parable. I pointed to the way Rembrandt depicts this moment the father first embraces the returning son. The son is kneeling before the father. The father's hands are on each of the younger son's shoulders.

Rembrandt's painting, however, is not necessarily depicting how the text of the parable is written. The parable never says the son fell on his knees or flat on the ground, though it is easy to imagine he did. The one who falls in the parable is the father!

Bernard Brandon Scott shows in English phrasing how the story may literally read in the original Greek language:

> Saw him his father did
> And moved to compassion
> And running fell on his neck
> And kissed him.

Scott says the first hearers of the parable were probably shocked by this loving response of embracing his son. Hearers might be pulled up short, Scott says, because they might have expected more from this father. More dignity, more discipline, more reverence, and more honor for the family.

Scott asks refreshing questions about the parables of Jesus and helps me reimagine each prodigal character. For example, in his book *Re-Imagine the World*, Scott says: "The son's reception is a dream come true. He has gotten away with it. He sinned against heaven and his father, and he's not going to be punished."[3] What will the neighbors say?

My friend John Mark Hicks says this idea that the son is not really repentant is not consistent with the declarations in the previous two parables about the high value heaven places on repentance. I still think the younger son repented. I imagine, however, that the younger prodigal was much like me and many humans I know—we live with a smirk on our faces thinking maybe we've gotten away with something.

Scott quotes a rabbinic anthology about the father's actions: "A king had a son who had gone astray from his father a journey of a hundred days; his friends said to him, 'Return to your father'; he said, 'I cannot.' Then his father sent to say, 'Return as far as you can, and I will come to you the rest of the way.' So God says, 'Return to me, and I will return to you.'"[4]

Though this is a favorite Christian story, Scott says something here that may blow your mind. "It is Christian antisemitism that sees this story only as the essence of the Gospel. This story was stolen from Israel." What does Scott mean by this bold statement? Here's how I understand what Scott is saying. Often, Christians think God got converted in the New Testament. To portray the teachings of Jesus as the first time God discovered grace and to caricature Jewish life as merely law-keeping legalism misses God's long-playing story that comes to us through millennia of love that culminates and is fulfilled in Jesus. Jesus continues but also reshapes ancient rabbinic tradition, telling stories of what God's love has always been like. God from the dawn of creation has been pursuing humanity. God is still pursuing us.

God is pursuing us like the father, who is portrayed as loving dirty sinners so much he doesn't wait to wash or baptize or dust anyone off before laying a big smooch on them. Scott says the Greek verb prefix for the word translated here as "kissed" indicates intensity, thus my justification for saying "big smooch."

It was this intensity that led to a powerful sermon about a kiss. On Sunday evening, March 29, 1891, Charles H. Spurgeon preached a sermon about the younger son at the Metropolitan Tabernacle in London. He quoted Master Trapp who said the father was within his rights to run to the son and kick him. There are such fathers in the world, both then and now, whose first and only response is retaliation toward a wayward child.

Yet the story takes a surprising twist for the first hearers, and for us when we hear it again with fresh ears—visualize it with a fresh mind's eye. The father kissed his younger son. Spurgeon preached a whole sermon on this kiss. His Bible translation in those days read, "He fell on his neck, and kissed him." Spurgeon interpreted that the father kissed him repeatedly, eagerly, much.

Spurgeon asks what all this kissing means. "When sinners come to God," Spurgeon said, God "gives them a loving reception, and a hearty welcome. If any one of you, while I am speaking, shall come to God, expecting mercy because of the great sacrifice of Christ, this shall be true of you as it has been true of many of us: 'He kissed him much.'" With each kiss, Spurgeon says, the father gives love, forgiveness, joy, and assurance.[5]

Before the COVID-19 pandemic, when I visited the sick, I would often kiss a friend or family member on the top of the head in their hospital bed, tell them God loves them, and sometimes sing them a hymn. During the worst of the pandemic, medical workers often provided affection and assurance to patients who were dying without the presence of family members.

My grandparents, parents, siblings, children, and in-laws often kiss on the cheek, forehead, or the side of the neck while hugging. A family kiss is an almost quiet expression of affection, compassion, joy, and assurance. From the first telling of the parable by Jesus, to Spurgeon, to Volf, this kiss and embrace have sparked continued theological imagining about the passion of welcoming sinners, even enemies, back home. The father has run, and now he embraces the younger son. The father shows his love in action before either speaks. When words fail us, much love is expressed with a kiss and embrace.

Prodigal Prayer

God, how can I embrace a četnik? How can I embrace people I hate, who reject your love or hurt the ones I love?

16

Forgive

The son said to him, "Father, I have sinned against heaven and against you. I am no longer worthy to be called your son."

A few years ago, I wrote a book, titled *Lay Down Your Guns*, about a doctor in Honduras who founded medical clinics in the mountains then defended them against the onslaught of drug cartels that threatened to destroy them. One of the subplots in this true story about Dr. Amanda Madrid was about the relationship she had with her mother, Maria Antonia, and her father, Florencio.

The reason I included Amanda's relationship with her parents was to show how she learned compassion, courage, and faith to do the things she did later, like facing down drug lords. Maria Antonia supported her daughter's dream to go to medical school, even after Florencio had rejected the idea. She listened closely to Amanda's plans and firmly guided her to be wise in the big city of Tegucigalpa. With a mix of love and resolve, she would complete medical school and serve for decades as a doctor to low-income and rural Hondurans who would otherwise be without a doctor.

As a teenager, Amanda had resented her father and his church. For Amanda, her church experience could be summed up in one word: *Prohibido!* Forbidden! Even if she was elected in the contest, "Queen of the Barrio," her father forbade her from attending the ceremony. She was forbidden from having a Quinceañera, a rite-of-passage fifteenth birthday party, like many girls in her neighborhood had. A lay pastor in an evangelical church, Florencio even forbade young Amanda from participating in passion plays and anything sponsored by the Catholic Church.

Amanda felt she had to be perfect in church because Florencio was a church leader. She could not wear makeup or earrings because these were considered by her church to be sinful adornments, unbecoming of a young woman. Pants were also questionable for girls in 1970s Honduras. Amanda, however, had a pair of neon-green pants she really liked.

"You may not wear those pants in church," Florencio said.

"What's wrong with wearing pants in church?" Amanda asked.

"It's wrong."

"Where does the Bible say that?" Amanda shot back.

Florencio read a Scripture from the book of Deuteronomy about women not wearing men's clothes and men not wearing women's clothes.

"Now," Florencio continued, "do you think you will wear those pants to church?"

The verse confused Amanda. How could her neon-green pants have anything to do with a man's clothes? No man would want to wear these green pants! Amanda stayed quiet, pausing the argument for the moment. But she had a secret plan.

The day of the next church gathering, Amanda put on her green pants, and after her father was already standing in front of the congregation to preach, she walked down the center aisle to the front row and sat down. Her green pants seemed to glow. She pursed her lips, squinted her eyes slightly, crossed her legs, and glared at her father.

Defiant, Amanda stiffened her body and steadied herself for her father to call her out publicly. Florencio did not, however, call out his daughter. He did not stop midsentence. He did not send Amanda out of church and back home to change.

Instead, Florencio continued to preach. Amanda, meanwhile, sat wondering what her papa thought, what he might say later. Her father did not satisfy Amanda with a response to her green-pants rebellion. Time passed, and Amanda could not let it go. She finally asked her father what he thought. Florencio said, "My Princess, I would rather have you in church wearing green pants than outside the church because I forced you to wear a dress."

What a surprise her father's response was to Amanda! She had expected to create a scene, but instead her independence, church participation, and fashion sense were all affirmed at one time! Sometimes we get a shocking reversal of expectations from our parents.

When the younger son returns home, he receives this stunning reversal of his expectations. The father does not respond as the son had expected. Had the son expected his father to run to him? Had he expected kisses? I don't imagine he did. He expects to be disowned. Such was this sense of shame that even after the father runs to the younger son and embraces him, the younger son still felt he must deliver his prepared speech: "Father, I have sinned against heaven and against you. I am no longer worthy to be called your son."

The younger son's speech did not come out as completely as he had rehearsed it. There was to be more, but that's all he got out. Like Florencio, the father with two sons does not address the younger son's message in the expected way. And like Amanda, the younger son would be surprised to hear how his father chose to respond. I'll address the father's response in the next chapter, but I want to explore the son's confession first. This confession may be one of the most poignant in scripture, partly because it is so rare and difficult, and partly because it seems to be the kind of attitude that opens the door for the father's response.

A child knowing she or he has messed up and actually saying so to parents is so rare. I have given a few speeches to my father in my twenties and thirties, and few, if any, involved *my* sins. This confession is not as easy as it sounds. Not many children think of saying "I'm sorry," confessing sin—much less do they say it aloud to their parents.

In fact, the words "I have sinned" are so infrequent even in scripture that only a handful of people ever make the confession. Lots of people say, "Have mercy on me!" but only a few, like a tax collector and the younger son, add that they are sinners.

When Judas sees Jesus bound up and condemned to execution, he says to the chief priests and the elders, "I have sinned, for I have betrayed innocent blood." Judas had betrayed Jesus for thirty pieces of silver. The religious leaders were indifferent to Judas. They said, "What is that to us? That's your responsibility." The narration then says, "So Judas threw the money into the temple and left. Then he went away and hanged himself."

Like Judas, the younger son had betrayed his family for money. When he came home, he was filled with remorse. Both the story of the younger son and the story of Judas betraying Jesus have fundamental themes of sin, betrayal, remorse, and absolution. A key difference, however, is that the younger son has come to his senses, turns on his remorse, and asks his father to forgive him.

We've all rehearsed speeches to wrongdoers or for wrongs we've done. What do we do with these speeches? How many of them ever get delivered? Some of them get half tried, hinted at, joked about, used as occasional emotional darts, and distilled into glaring looks. Rarely do these fantasized speeches exit our mouths as rehearsed. Often, the speeches we actually give are worse than the ones we rehearsed, rarely better.

I'm all for a dialogue and needing to say things to one another. It's just that working ourselves into a one-way speech or text is rarely a good format for approaching someone. I've rehearsed many speeches to have with people in my first fifty years of life. Through coaching from counselors and life experience, I don't practice and deliver too many speeches anymore. When we regularly say only what love requires at the time, pent-up speeches become less necessary.

Short as the speech is, the father interrupts his son. We're surprised again when the sequence the son and hearers of the parable expect is upended in the meeting of the father and son. The son confesses sin against heaven and the father, says he's no longer worthy, but the rest of his speech—the part about being considered like a hired worker—doesn't get delivered. The father interrupts the confession; he doesn't seem to need more.

I wonder if the father needed *any* of his son's speech. The return and holding the son in the father's arms seem to be enough.

Do you have a recurring speech for someone you could release in a healthier way than rehearsing it repeatedly in your mind? Does your speech include a confession? Where and to whom do you need to perform your speech? In our imagined speeches, we often prepare and attempt to protect ourselves from imagined angry interruptions to our speeches. You might also be ready for part of your speech to be cut short by a loved one's mercy.

Prodigal Prayer

Holy One, I am thankful for wise mentors and counselors who helped me learn what it means to be a prodigal. I am a striving, struggling, growing, fallibly faithful child of God redeemed by the ransoming and deeply loving work of Jesus Christ in death, resurrection, and eternal reign.

17

Robe

But the father said to his servants, "Quick! Bring the best robe and put it on him. Put a ring on his finger and sandals on his feet."

Max Lucado tells a story about a single widower named Joe who had a daughter named Madeline. From the time Madeline was a little girl, she and her poppa would dance every Christmas Eve. As Madeline grew older and taller, she could dance looking eye to eye with her father.

When she was a teenager, they did not see eye to eye about piercings or how she dressed. Most of all, they did not agree on her hanging out with the lanky, tattooed kid from down the street. One Christmas Eve, with family gathered at his mother's house, music playing, Joe asked Madeline, "Would you dance with your poppa tonight?" Joe reached out his hand and Madeline brushed it aside, rejecting her poppa for a Christmas Eve dance for the first time in seventeen years.

Months passed with more of the same, and Madeline decided to leave home. Her boyfriend's cousin in a faraway city had promised to give them a place to stay. Two bus tickets and newfound freedom felt almost as intoxicating as their regular partying. After a few weeks, the cousin grew tired of these freeloaders and kicked them out. That night they slept at a shelter. Madeline's boyfriend announced the next morning that he would be hitchhiking back home. Madeline did not want to go home, so she stayed at the shelter, alone.

With no money and no place to go, Madeline met another teenager who showed a wad of tips she'd made dancing in a club. "Think about it," her new friend said, then texted her the address to the strip club. Madeline did not want to think about it and spent the next few days looking for other work until she was exhausted, hungry, and completely broke. Her hands shaking, she texted her new friend and asked if they could meet at the club.

Madeline danced because she was hungry and needed a steady place to live. Soon she would be rooming with her friend, dancing, eating better, and trying not to think about her poppa and what he would think about all this.

After Madeline's ex-boyfriend had returned to her hometown, he had spilled information to her poppa about where Madeline lived and hinted at how she was making money. He also gave Joe his cousin's mailing address.

One day, after several months passed, Madeline's ex-boyfriend's cousin walked into the club. He'd been tracking her for some time. The cousin was exasperated to be receiving daily mail from Madeline's "Poppa," and would she please tell whoever was sending this mail where she lived? He handed her a stack of envelopes, all the same size and color. She stuffed them in her purse and asked for a ride back to her apartment.

At first, a mix of shame and self-protection prevented Madeline from opening the envelopes from home. She stacked the letters in a shoebox and pushed them under her bed and tried to forget about them; but she couldn't. As Christmas approached, she thought about her poppa and the unopened envelopes.

Alone in her apartment the week before Christmas, Madeline finally pulled out the shoebox and opened the first card from her poppa.

"I know where you are," her poppa had written on the first card. "I know what you do. This does not change the way I feel about you."

Tears streamed down Madeline's face as she read each sentence. One last line—a question her father asked on the card—caught her breath, and Madeline started sobbing. Trembling hands, wiping tears, she opened card after card from her father, and they all included the same three sentences then ended with the same question for her.

She booked a bus ticket, looking at the date, and thought she just might make it for Christmas. She would answer her poppa's question in person. After a day-long bus ride, Madeline stood on the front porch of her father's home and rang the doorbell. Joe opened the door to see his daughter holding a backpack in one hand and a card in the other.

Standing eye to eye again, Madeline broke the stunned silence.

"The answer is yes," she said. "If the invitation is still good, the answer is yes."

Tears welled up in Joe's eyes and he said, "Oh my, the invitation is still good."

And so the two danced again on Christmas Eve.

On the floor, near the door, lay a card with Madeline's name and her father's request: "Will you come home and dance again with your poppa?"[1]

Like Lucado's story, the parable of Jesus includes a father who does something surprising and remarkable. The reflexive response of some parents to a prodigal is to ask questions and make new ground rules for the wayward child. Susan Eastman says when she first taught on the parable of prodigals in a church, she was a young mother. She could not imagine the tensions of parent and child that would come in later years, but older parents in the church could. Eastman innocently asked, "What would you do if this were your child?" She was surprised at the responses.

One mother said she'd make her wayward child sign on to new house rules! Another parent said, he'd let him in but there'd be hell to pay! Eastman writes, "Clearly, throwing a party was the last thing on their minds. I was astounded." She contrasts these responses with God's "economics of grace," asking, what are we to make of such prodigal generosity that defies all parental common sense? Eastman says the means of forgiveness and reconciliation is the gift of relationship the father offers the returning son. Will the younger son accept this abundance of love or live in shame the rest of his life? Will the elder son accept the economics of grace, welcoming his brother home, or will the elder brother believe there must be winners and losers in a zero-sum game? The economics of the kingdom are not about what is earned or deserved by younger or elder siblings but what is freely given and freely received.[2]

Now it is the father's turn to say something about the son's return. He is about to show how God's economics of grace play out.

The father interrupts the younger son, and he doesn't even speak to the son directly but says, "Servants! Bring my best clothes; put them on my son."

The father does not ask for an accounting. He does not appeal to the rules of inheritance. He believes there is enough love, blessing, and forgiveness to go around. The questions many parents want to ask are of no concern to the father here. Some of us want at least to talk about what happened. If nothing else, we want to ask neutral questions like, "How was the far country? Where exactly did you go?" The father asks no such questions but instead immediately calls for clothes for the long-lost son. If the child is dressed in rags and half naked, it's easy to understand the desire to clothe the son, to bring a robe.

Parents and children often talk past one another, not responding to what the other is saying or feeling. It's a conversation of non sequiturs. Why doesn't the father respond to what the son is saying? He could have said, "How did this happen, son? What sins against heaven and me? And what's all this about worthiness?" Much parental energy goes toward defining terms of how the child is going to pay back the debt. Not this father.

The son did not get the rest of his speech out—the part about serving with the hired hands. The father is more interested in the symbols of welcome. What do all these things mean to the father? "Bring the best robe," would show the son, the family, and the neighbors that he truly remains a family member. A twinge of "you better not waste these gifts this time" seems nowhere to be found in the father's voice. He goes on calling for a ring for the son's finger. The ring might say to everyone watching, "This is still my son."

Offering the ring, the robe, the shoes confers on the son a new identity. Instead of not worthy, the father rearranges how he views his son. The son is known again as "son of mine" to the father.

The mother is backstage in the story, but I imagine her telling the servants to be sure to get a basin, water, soap, lots of scrubbing cloth. "Hurry," I can imagine her saying. "Help him wash before he puts on the best robe." She is carrying olive oil to anoint her son's chapped hands before they slip on the ring. Before the shoes are placed on her son's feet, the loving mother will be sure his cracked feet are cleaned with the pedicuring tools of their day.

What do you imagine about this story in your life? Depending on your situation and stage in life, you might identify with this loving mother who washes her children's crusty feet. You may identify with the father who is willing to welcome in a prodigal way, lavishly. You may identify as a younger son or daughter who, like Madeline, has been far away much too long. The story of prodigals is your story, too. How many cards, texts, or signs from heaven will it take for you to plan on going home for Christmas?

18

Celebrate

Bring the fattened calf and kill it. Let's have a feast and celebrate.

Phillip Yancey in his book *What's So Amazing About Grace* tells a story about a woman in Boston who used her agency and power to transform a moment of disappointment into a celebration.

The woman was engaged to be married and planned a reception at a fancy hotel. She put down a deposit of $13,000 for the reception.

As the wedding came closer, the groom got cold feet and broke off their engagement. The bride asked the hotel for her deposit back and discovered the hard definition of *nonrefundable*.

She had at least two choices, and both involved eating. She could eat the loss of money and not have the party. Or she could eat the loss of money and go forward with the party. On the night she was to be married, she instead welcomed hungry people on the streets of Boston to a party.

Like the father in the parable, the bride had been betrayed. And like the father, even though she faced lost resources, this did not deter her from celebrating. The woman paid for servers to dish up hors d'oeuvres to senior citizens, people with addictions, and those without a secure base to call home. They sipped champagne, ate chocolate cake, and danced late into the night. People accustomed to dumpster diving dined on chicken cordon bleu. The hostess and would-be bride made sure the menu, in mock honor of the groom, was chicken. And of course, it was boneless.

Just like the woman in Boston, so the father has choices about how to respond to the situation in front of him. He could turn the son out to live with the hired workers, as the son had expected he would. He could set some new house rules. He could deliver "I told you so" speeches and reprimands. In response to his son's return, however, the father says, "Get the fatted calf and kill it, and let us eat and celebrate."

From the number of stories we have of Jesus around tables, Jesus loved to celebrate. We could use the word "party," because the occasions Jesus attended were not all religious celebrations. Jesus partied with people the religious considered untouchable sinners. One example was when Jesus's friend Matthew, who worked as a tax collector for the IRS (that's Israel Revenue Service, benefiting the Romans), wanted to introduce all his rowdy friends to Jesus. So Matthew threw a party, and Jesus attended (Mark 2:15–16).

Jesus made a habit of hanging out with sinners and eating with them, which was frowned upon by the religious establishment. They began grumbling and saying, "He associates with, even eats with, sinners." While Jesus is the "life of the party," those who are the "death of the party" stay aloof and give it the stink eye. Death dealers critique food, music, dancing, and social associations to fit neatly into their sexism, racism, classism, religionism. When we read "party with," we do well to read, "be in the same church with" and "fight for the rights of" and "eat with at a potluck or taco truck."

On the same occasion, as told in the Gospel of Matthew, Jesus asks the party police, "Who needs a doctor? Healthy people or sick people?" (Matt. 9:12). Jesus treated sick sinners like a healing doctor who also loved to party.

In Luke's telling about this party, Jesus tells three stories, and the punch line story is about prodigals. All three stories involve lost valuables being found. The lost son takes this one step further: not just lost but dead and now found alive! All three stories involve throwing parties to celebrate the finding of the valuables, most importantly finding lost children of God! What this shows me is that the parable parallels Jesus's life. Jesus loved to party. Jesus loved to party with sinners. Jesus loved to show party poopers how to party with sinners.

Jesus tells another story about a wealthy man who invited friends to his house for a big party. All his friends sent their regrets, complete with excuses. Frustrated, the rich man ordered his entourage to invite the poor. The rich man's staff did not know many poor people, so they half-filled the house with neighbors. When the rich man noticed the house was half empty, he ordered his staff to pick up homeless people begging for money at the street corners with cardboard signs. They did this, and soon poor people filled the rich man's house. They partied like it was 1999, eating and drinking, dancing, and jumping into the swimming pool with their clothes on. I made up that last part about jumping in the pool, but that really happened on *La La Land*—and once or twice when I was in high school. Was this parable an inspiration for the Boston bride inviting the poor to eat a $13,000 meal?

One day in 1988, this story Jesus told changed the course of my life together with my fiancée. Jill and I had attended a conference on missions and were reading in the Gospels this story of the banquet where everyone gave excuses why they could not come to party with the rich man. At the time, we were considering going on a six-week mission internship, but we wanted to get married and did not know if it was wise to do both. We were bound and determined to get married. We weren't bound and determined to go on a six-week mission trip. One of the excuses given in the parable of the wealthy man and the party is that someone was recently married and declined to attend the party.

This story became what I later learned from one of my seminary professors, Everett Huffard, to call a "word check" in our lives. A word check is when a hockey player skates out of the Bible story and "checks" you, and you go flying into the wall of the ice rink. Rather not be checked into the wall by a hockey player? Okay, let's say the Bible story "checks" your heart, your motives. A word check sometimes knocks you off an unwise or even deadly path and offers you a course correction. This story changed the course of our lives because we realized we could go on the mission trip if we changed our wedding date.

We did change the date of the wedding in order to go on the six-week internship. Our parents made sacrifices and changes as well. This meant we would travel to Kenya just ten days after our wedding—a honeymoon, of sorts, in East Africa! That trip led us to join a mission team and to live in Uganda from 1994 to 2001. This parable Jesus told about participating in the extravagant love of the banquet of God changed our lives. We joined the party.

Could you celebrate with fellow prodigals in Boston without trying to solve homelessness that evening? Can you be friends with someone who is in a completely different place in life, poorer or richer than you, an immigrant, a different political party or disposition, even someone you may judge as a law breaker, a sinner?

19

Alive

"For this son of mine was dead and is alive again; he was lost and is found." So they began to celebrate.

One of the best speeches I ever heard was delivered by a man who made it his life mission to see the walking dead return to life. Bryan Stevenson's work has become more broadly known after actor Michael B. Jordan starred as Stevenson in the critically acclaimed movie *Just Mercy*.

The film dramatizes the true story of Walter McMillian, a young man who was sentenced to die for a notorious murder he did not commit. McMillian's case led a young Stevenson to death row in Alabama to confront systems of injustice. As an attorney for the vulnerable and wrongly convicted, Stevenson has faced opposition from district attorneys, police, prosecutors, and judges, and his exoneration work has put him face-to-face with prisoners on death row.

From 1973 until October 5, 2022, 1,548 people have been executed in the United States. In the same time period, 190 people have been exonerated and released from death row. Most of those exonerations have happened because of organizations like Equal Justice Initiative (EJI), which Stevenson founded in 1989.[1] How do they do it?

Stevenson and the EJI staff get proximate to the walking dead and learn their stories. They serve clients who often cannot pay, researching and filing appeals in cases where false accusations and official misconduct have led to wrongful convictions. EJI offers hope for the walking dead to rise again and go free.

In the parable, we hear the father twice say his son was dead. Death, however, is not the identity the father is wishing on the son. We get the sense the father is not speaking this as a curse but as a reality of the son's existence. Had he come to believe the son was truly dead? No biblical story, certainly not this one, teaches us to say, "This child is dead to me." The father does not say anything like that.

Now in this scene of the parable, the father exults in the fact that his son was dead but now alive! Further, just as family members and defenders of death row inmates, the father in the parable has a flexible relationship that is willing to transform into a new identity with the son. No giving up. He is father of a son who was on death row and is now free!

Only a handful of people in all of time and creation have ever seen something that was dead be reanimated and brought back to life. These words of death and life will make more sense later in Luke's story, when something miraculous happens. Jesus was murdered by a torture method called crucifixion, buried in a tomb, then three days later rose from the dead, appeared fully alive to his disciples, and ascended to heaven where, I believe, he reigns and will judge evil doers and restore all creation and humanity when the time is right.

We can only imagine the deep disappointment of losing a Messiah who called you friend. He was supposed to save Israel from oppressors but died on an oppressor's execution cross. How did it feel to lose their only hope? Luke does not stumble onto these phrases. As a writer about redemption of Israel and the nations, Luke intentionally places map pins for points of reference.

The exclamation of the father would later be the exclamation of the disciples: "He was dead but he's now alive!"

We take risks to read the parable in ways that challenge us to interrupt death dealing with life-giving hope. Jesus taught about life and was sentenced to death. In every time and every society, death dealers always oppose life givers. There are grave risks to truly offering all people life and hope.

For Stevenson, life-giving means doing the arduous work to get people off death row. For my brother practicing medicine in New York and my sister-in-law working in the pregnancy care organization *Care Net*, life-giving means protecting both the rights of the unborn and the rights of women. For my wife, Jill, my daughter, Ashley, and my son, Jacob, teaching school is a life-giving way to equip students to make the world more just, peaceful, and hopeful. I have seen them and other family and friends who are teachers deeply love their students, enjoy and laugh with them, and prepare them to flourish. You couldn't pay most people to willingly enter a room daily with middle schoolers. Ashley gives life by teaching sixth graders joyfully and entertains us with quotes from her students, such as, "I hate this class but I like you." Ashley brings me life in our regular walks and dinners. She challenges us to read good books, love life to the fullest, and laugh often. I'm biased, but I believe our communities owe teachers a debt of gratitude and anything we can do to encourage them in the vital work of educating the next generations.

What does life-giving mean for you? The parable vividly describes a life-giving person who waits, hopes, runs, kisses, forgives, and restores life. The parable allows us to imagine a God who makes life in the places of death. We are called to do the same. Until the good news of this parable matters on death row, music row, cannery row, and skid row, it is not fully true for everyone.

The parable invites us to stand by the road and weep tears of reversal with the father. The parable calls us to stand by the road and identify with the prodigal crumpled in a heap on the path home. The parable invites us to stand by the road and identify with the mother waiting her turn to pick up the son and wrap him in her arms. The parable calls us into places of death to bring a message and healing presence of life.

"He was dead but he's now alive!"

20

Field

Meanwhile, the older son was in the field.

Ask my four older siblings, and they will tell you I got away with everything. Whatever. If that is true, it is because parents are compensating the youngest for all the grief elder siblings give the youngest like me. As Dr. Phil would say, having elder siblings is not something you cure; it is something you will always manage! You elder siblings get to be pioneers, but you were also your parents' experiments. We younger siblings are the exquisite products of refined parenthood.

My friend Wade preached a sermon from the perspective of the older brother. His first sermon move was to confess being an older brother. Young siblings might hear their confessions and forgive older siblings, for they knew not what they did. After all, the thumping and bullying—these were all in the elder sibling manual. You elder siblings were just following the rules, right? At least the oldest was.

Sometimes being oldest can be downright unbearable for you, I'm sure. You can imagine better than I can what it was like for the older brother in the story of Jesus when his younger brother came home. When your little brother finagled half the family farm then sold it and ran off with the money, you weren't surprised. He'd always been wild. Your father had always been way too lenient with him, always giving him the benefit of the doubt.

But you never did. After growing up sharing a room with your little brother, you knew exactly what kind of person he was. That's why, when he finally ran off, you thought, *Good riddance*. You were fairly confident, given the circumstances under which he left, he wouldn't be back.

In his absence, you had more of your father to yourself. You grew closer to each other. Now there was no doubt about who his favorite son was. You were his right-hand man.

The first line of the parable, "a man had two sons," now begins to make sense when the younger son returns and the elder son is nowhere to be found. He was putting in overtime on the family farm. The parable introduces him with this line: "Now the elder son was in the field."

Ever dutiful, the elder son stays home and works hard, never breaking any of the father's rules. With no radio to listen to on the tractor, and no tractor, the elder brother only had his thoughts in the field with him. The field is a good place to construct a narrative of self-merit and dutifulness. You're working harder than any other slackers, certainly harder than that squanderer who selfishly gutted the family business.

We too construct stories of our dutifulness in our work fields. "Why am I the only one who cares about this project enough to get stuff done?" Years ago, I helped plan a work project with a coworker. Our roles were not clearly defined, but we had trusted one another to pitch in our share. It seemed that where I was preparing with tasks for the event, my coworker was preparing with wishful thinking that all would go well. Though the project did go well, I could not step over my dutiful work to fully enjoy the accomplishment. I addressed my thoughts and feelings with my coworker. He was gracious, asked what he could have done, and requested that I make him aware of things he can do rather than taking them all on myself. I had allowed the dutiful underside to negatively impact my enjoyment of the event. No doubt I've been on the other side of this, where coworkers, friends, or family have felt I didn't pull my weight.

We also construct these narratives of our dutifulness at church: "I am serving and giving offerings, and more people need to be generous so this church will not have to struggle financially!" We might dutifully accept sinners into our church family because that's what God says to do, yet in our hearts continue to believe we are better than they are because we've never been addicted to drugs or divorced or promiscuous. We become like the elder brother in our fields, never noticing the joy of heaven that a sinner has come home.

We construct stories of dutifulness in our families: "Why do I have to always feed the dog and no one else will?!" or "Why don't my siblings come to the hospital to see Mom?"

We construct stories of our dutifulness to God, even sacrificial patriotism to a country where we live: "My hard-earned money goes to taxes for freeloaders!"

The elder brother is not the only one in left field over dutifulness. The story of the elder brother is the story of so many of us, including me, a confessed younger brother with some elder brother tendencies. Yet even skilled preachers and teachers may leave out the elder brother's part of the story. They may tell the story and end with the celebration of the father for the younger son. Forgetting or ignoring the rest of the story violates the story Jesus tells, leaving us with a half-truth, or less than half.

Another preacher buddy I know had focused his storytelling on the younger as prodigal so many times the story had lost a step for him. Then one Sunday, like my friend Wade, he preached from the point of view of the older brother. He realized during the sermon that he is the older brother. He became so emotional he could barely finish the sermon. What does such a realization of being an elder sibling really mean? I mean, all kidding aside, what's so bad about being an older sibling? At this point, he's just minding his business and working in the field. Soon, however, the elder brother will voice his concerns about his brother's return. That's what elder siblings do, right? He's a perfect stand-in for the concerns of hearers of the story like us. If I am being transparent, I'm concerned as well. How about you? Even before the elder brother opens his mouth, we're already wondering about the sanity of the father. *Are you kidding me? You're just going to throw a party for that squanderer?! You're okay with this? Are we not going to talk about this?*

Being an elder sibling means you raise questions! Nowhere in the story, says New Testament Scholar N. T. Wright, is it implied that the younger son's sinful actions are condoned. We'll soon learn what the brother thinks is condoning when he sees the ring, robe, and shoes and smells the roasted meat from the party in honor of the squirrelly squanderer.

There is no issue with someone being older or younger. I wonder if the core of the issue for the elder brother is that he has never left home. He thinks home is about maintaining rules, inheritance traditions, and duty. Because he has never left home, ironically, he cannot understand that home is also about prodigious love, forgiveness, joy, and abundant grace, even for those who mess up royally.

The younger brother did something Jesus required of his followers: to leave home, family even. Granted, the younger brother was not on the kind of mission to seek and save the lost that the disciples of Jesus were undertaking. The way of Jesus is resolute and not always moving the same direction as our families. Following Jesus may bring family conflict and divisions. We cannot always reconcile our biological family with the life of following Jesus. Some must part ways with their biological family, others their social, cultural, or political groups or views, to follow Jesus.

Jesus shows us that it is possible to break with family but still find ways to be faithful to them, love them, and receive love from them. Mary the mother of Jesus was the Lord's first and most faithful follower. Yet Jesus resisted his family's tug back to "sanity" when they thought he was crazy. Jesus said his true family are those who listen and do what he teaches. In this book's close reading of the greatest parable Jesus ever told, I've chosen to feature my own family stories alongside the parable family and other fiction and nonfiction family stories. I want to show how family tension and loyalty may coexist and urge you to reflect on your own prodigal experiences in wider terms than the centuries of interpreting this parable simply as a patriarch waiting on a wayward son to come home. The diverse and inclusive ways to read and discern this parable have only been hinted at in these chapters, and you as a reader may take it further into your own experience.

Jesus did not ask us to do anything he did not, himself, do. He left the heaven of relationship with our great Creator and Spirit, the one he often called Father. He came to earth in body as a mix of God and humanity we can never fully understand or explain. Jesus left home. The way Jesus decided to come home was to first leave home, to become a prodigal wanderer. This sojourning Jesus inspired and invited not only wandering, squandering Jews to follow the Messiah but also for every wayward and wily nation of prodigals to follow as well.

The younger son became a prodigal who left home then returned. The father became a prodigal who did something extravagant and illogical to welcome home a squanderer without conditions. The elder brother, meanwhile, refused to leave the home he had always known. The elder brother was a prodigal on his own land.

Miroslav Volf says, "The world of fixed rules and stable identities is the world of the older brother." What is the world of the father and how is it different? The father adjusts to the complexities of each of the brother's lives, willing to take on new identities, such as "father of the lost sons."

Are you willing to take on the identity of "mother of a daughter who had an abortion"? Are you willing to take on the identity of "father of a son in prison"? Are you willing to take on the identity of "mother of a daughter who is going through a divorce"? Are you aware you can take on the identity of a parent whose child is transgender and still show deep, deep love for your child? Have you considered that the way you think of fixed rules, church, and ethics may not be the world in which you will now best show love to your child?

The father is willing to shape-shift and take on the identity of a father of a prodigal squanderer, and the father has the wisdom and flexibility to take on the identity of a father of a resistant, selfish, arrogant son who refuses to love the younger son. So much does the father take on this identity that he pleads with the elder son. Volf says the father even "draws his older son's anger upon himself" and thus destabilizes his own world.

The father's commitment, says Volf, "is not to rules and given identities but to his sons whose lives are too complex to be regulated by fixed rules and whose identities are too dynamic to be defined once for all." Does this mean the father gives up on rules, becomes completely uninterested in the heritage, inheritance, rules? No.

Volf writes,

> Yet he does not give up the rules and the order. Guided by the indestructible love which makes space in the self for others in their alterity, which invites the others who have transgressed to return, which creates hospitable conditions for their confession, and rejoices over their presence, the father keeps re-configuring the order without destroying it so as to maintain it as an order of embrace rather than exclusion.[1]

The father, says Volf, simply does not allow the moral rules to rule. Rules do not regulate relationship. He refuses to construct an identity in exclusion of the sons. Relationship is the priority, not the rules, even if breaking the rules is the way to begin healing broken relationships.

The father's love is indestructible, so it can shift and change to the needs of the sons. He sacrifices his own vision, his own rules for the sake of the sons, to bring them back to himself but also to one another. The father's flexible, loving identity is not a violence of exclusion but an order of embrace.

Prodigal Prayer

In the field, we can become isolated and joyless and merciless. Because of this, in order to nurture and renew my imagination for the internal life of compassion and mercy, I have some routine weekly practices of prayer and some annual practices. During Lent, for example, I often read a quirky book by Edward Hayes titled *A Lenten Hobo Honeymoon: Daily Reflections for the*

Journey of Lent. In the reflection on the fourth Sunday of Lent, Hayes says homecoming is only an event for those who leave home. Hayes says, "The older brother questions his father's love for him. The younger brother has left home and so can return. He knows of the fullness of his father's love, which is both unconditional and lavish."[2]

21

Observer

When he came near the house, he heard music and dancing.

In early 2020, I resigned as minister of a church in Tulsa, Oklahoma. At the same time, a global pandemic shut down large gatherings, including church services and the funeral for my father. Rather than being insiders of a church, my wife and I were now outside looking in, like millions of others "attending" church online. When churches returned to in-person services a few months later, we began visiting churches with our adult children in their new hometowns and with friends in Tulsa.

The experience of visiting unfamiliar churches is not always enjoyable and can make a guest feel like an observer. At the same time, however, we have enjoyed observing a variety of music, liturgy, race, culture, and leadership in churches. Jill and I have decided to join a church together that is mutually agreeable to us. No rushing one another to something that fits only convenience, superficial preferences, or expedience. We are looking for a church that worships and honors God and is inclusive of all people—a church for prodigals like us.

At this point in the parable, point of view changes to the elder brother. Working in the fields, the elder brother hears the sounds of a party, and it seems no one has invited him. He is an observer on the outside looking in. The perspective invites us to stand with the elder brother and listen to the music and see the flickering lights and dancing figures in the distance. Only you can remember or name how you have been or are currently on the outside looking in. This can happen in family relationships, in a church, at work, on social media, at school. What does it feel like to hear music and see dancing at a party you are observing from the outside?

This raw feeling of being on the outs is palpable. As the elder son approaches the house, can he smell the roasted meat? Can he see smoke from the barbecue pit as he approaches from the fields? Does he imagine the fatted calf is roasting now on his industrious behalf? He is so valuable, surely the party is in his honor, and they'd gone ahead because they wanted to surprise him!

The fiction of the parable's elder brother being on the outs of a party now intersects with the true story of religious experts objecting to Jesus's partying with sinners. Feasting with sinners is precisely what started all this storytelling about lost money and celebration, a lost lamb and a shepherd who celebrates the find. So when Jesus tells this trilogy of stories, the climax is here with the introduction of the elder son and what he decides to do. The elder brother is like those staying aloof from sinners where Jesus was the life of the party. The elder brother at this point is an observer and not participating in that life.

The actions of Jesus and the parable overlay with our own stories and pose a question. The question is not so much, "Will we welcome the kinds of people Jesus welcomed?" Certainly we should. But the more difficult question for me is, "What makes me think I am welcomed by Jesus and others are unwelcomed in the first place?"

What compels us to move from being self-righteous observers to fellow prodigals at the table with Jesus? Henri Nouwen said,

> As I reflect on my own journey, I become more and more aware of how long I have played the role of observer. For years I had instructed students on the different aspects of the spiritual life, trying to help them see the importance of living it. But had I, myself, really ever dared to step into the center, kneel down, and let myself be held by a forgiving God?[1]

My wife and I are looking for a church not for observers but for fellow prodigals. I understand there are many churches like this, and I am grateful for your invitations into these communities. As of this writing, we are not members of a specific church. We do not believe there is a perfect church and know well that we are flawed people who will be with other flawed people. We believe God will lead us to this place.

How is the search going for you? You may not want exactly what I want in a church. You may be looking for companionship on life's journey, for beautiful music, for challenging preaching, for deepening your faith, for a community that serves the homeless population, for a substance abuse program. Some people who attend church regularly realize they need the habit of kneeling in a worshipping community, confessing sins, living in relationships of accountability.

Some church attenders view those not attending church as prodigals. They may think of themselves as non-prodigals because they attend church. The line of thinking is that if you do not attend church, you are a prodigal or on your way to becoming one.

Possibilities such as a spiritual search outside the walls of formal church membership are not usually accepted or respected.

Meanwhile, many who are considered "prodigals" avoid church attendance because of the rhetoric, culture, and belief system of many Christian churches that have woven politics into their teachings and practices. They hear the discordant music and have no interest in entering that party. Tens of millions of people believe in God and identify as Christians but do not want to enter the party at churches where it seems the cost of admission is to vote a certain way. They do not believe churches when they say they are not political yet send clear political signals in sermons, programs, church rhetoric, conversations, and expectations. Mahatma Gandhi is credited with saying, "Those who believe religion and politics aren't connected don't understand either." Politics by definition simply means what one does in the "polis," or the public square, or city-state. A church that displays an American flag or honors the military is making a political decision. A church that is active in immigration reform is making a political decision. Christianity is not necessarily for a certain American political party, but Christianity is indeed political when we act publicly in these ways. Rather than assuming God is on the side of our particular politics, why not seriously ask how Jesus interacted and was impacted by the politics of his times? Wasn't it religious and political leaders who crucified Jesus, who was a political threat to them?

I have heard Christians say "keep politics out of the church" yet post social media ideology that is one click away from hate speech. Deeply flawed American two-party politics must not shape our faith. Our faith in Jesus must reshape our politics, or how we live in the world and enact life.

We each have a decision to make about how we live our lives, how we approach neighbors, strangers, and enemies.

Self-proclaimed non-prodigals like the elder brother have rules that certain people are not allowed inside where they live and worship. Prodigals often stand outside looking in and do not want to enter a party with "non-prodigals" anyway. What can be done about this impasse?

When we look from the outside in, we may be drawn into some Christian communities. We can decide not to play the role of observers. We may hear the sweet sounds of partying and want in. The empty feeling of being outside a party can defeat us or it can be used as a space of change in our lives. Worldwide, there are many Christian communities worth entering, worth dancing with to the rhythm of the good news of Jesus Christ.

Tim Keller says elder siblings need to take a serious look in the mirror, because Jesus aimed the parable primarily at Pharisees and called them to change. He says a huge difference in the two brothers is the younger knew he was alienated from the father and the elder did not. Jesus said the sick need a doctor, but the elder brother doesn't think he's sick. The younger siblings of the world, says Keller, can easily see why the younger brother left in the first place. Keller says, "There are many people today who have abandoned any kind of religious faith because they see clearly that the major religions are simply full of elder brothers. . . . Everybody knows that the Christian gospel calls us away from the licentiousness of younger brotherness, but few realize that it also condemns moralistic elder brotherness."[2]

For those who have ears to hear, a breath is pulled and held while we wait for the response of the elder brother. Will he stay outside or enter the party? The elder brother has some questions of his own.

22

What

So he called one of the servants and asked him what was going on. "Your brother has come," he replied, "and your father has killed the fattened calf because he has him back safe and sound."

When I first heard about the 1921 Tulsa Massacre, my mind was consumed with one big question: *What's going on?* This one question led me to engage in conversations about the roots and ongoing harm of racial injustices and inequities in health, education, incarceration, and housing in Tulsa. Marvin Gaye asked a question to protest war in the 1970s, and his question is still operative for lament and protest today. *What's going on?*

When I began asking the question about racism in Tulsa, I learned White mobs, many deputized and armed by Tulsa Police Department, killed an estimated three hundred Black people on June 1, 1921, according to then Red Cross Director Maurice Willows.[1] Thirty-five blocks of more than one hundred

Black-owned businesses, two dozen churches, a hospital, a school, a library, and 1,256 Black-owned homes were burned to ashes in one day.

This is still living history, with three survivors remaining in Tulsa and thousands of descendants of the massacre. For the first time ever, I wanted to know what I could do to help survivors and descendants of the 1921 Tulsa Massacre to atone for a horrible, local, communal sin. I thought, if White people burned down homes and businesses, White people should also help rebuild homes and businesses.

For one hundred years, no reparations or settlements have ever been paid for losses of life and property in the Greenwood community. Asking *What's going on?* led my family to establish a nonprofit to make reparations through increasing home ownership and investment for Black families in Tulsa. This work of reparation arose by asking the same question the elder brother asked and taking time to listen to the voices of those experiencing racial trauma.

The elder brother asks the question of a servant in his father's house. Hearing the music, smelling the roasting fatted calf, seeing the dancing, the elder brother asked, "What's going on?"

The servant's reply must have stung the elder brother. "Your brother has come, and your father has killed the fatted calf because he has him back safe and sound." Why at this point would any of us not side with the elder brother? He faithfully served his family. He has an honest question about what is happening.

In fairness to the elder brother, he had done nothing whatsoever wrong at this point and had been a dutiful and faithful family member. The brother is like so many of us when we see something that doesn't seem right. We want to know, *What's going on?*

When we assume we already know what's going on, inaction, mercilessness, and injustice may prevail. I have heard many times over how White people claim their ancestors were not slaveholders, or in Tulsa, their grandparents were not part of the 1921 massacre. Instead of asking, *What's going on?* and learning more from the perspectives of those suffering racial trauma, the claim "I wasn't there" is an attempt to absolve ourselves of any guilt or responsibility for racial healing and reconciliation. I have talked with dozens of Black Tulsans who carry this racial trauma and pain. The kind of continued claim of color blindness and denial that racism exists is part of the long history of denial found in systemic White supremacy.

The brother's question is the opposite of this kind of denial. *What's going on?* is a question that may be used constructively. If we are willing to listen to voices unlike our own, the question can powerfully change our local communities. I am learning to ask what's going on in my local community. Where has death dealing brought human harm and destruction? Where has life giving brought human flourishing and the love of God in my community? Further, what can I do to interrupt those ways of death and rebuild ways of life? Theologian Kelly Brown Douglas calls this kind of attentiveness and action "resurrection reparations."

So, in the work of our nonprofit, we do resurrection reparations with Black homeowners who have faced historic and current discrimination in housing. In visiting with Black families regularly, we ask, *What's going on?* We discuss options for their home repair and how to solidify generational home ownership for their family. We decide together which contractor and bids they can trust, and most often we contract with Black-owned businesses.

Drawing from generous donors to the nonprofit 1256 Movement, we then agree with the homeowner and contractor to pay up to $10,000 of remodeling repairs or a down payment assistance for a new home. We named the nonprofit 1256 Movement because we are committed over ten years to reparations for 1,256 family homes, since the same number of Black-owned homes were burned down by White mobs in the 1921 massacre.

I'm grateful to my mother, Charlotte Taylor, who helped start this fund for reparations as a memorial after my dad's death. My wife, Jill, my brothers, Brent and Toby, and friends Amber and Chuck Oputa have helped me form a board and launch this nonprofit to practice reparations through increased home ownership for Black families in Tulsa. This project is a modest contribution compared to the historic and ongoing work of activists, journalists, and civic and faith leaders who have done the historic and current work of calling out and exposing White supremacy, greed, and denial of the harm done.

If you have questions related to the topic of reparations, you can learn more about the nonprofit at www.1256movement.org. A portion of the proceeds from this book will support 1256 Movement.

Prodigal Prayer

What's going on? What is happening in my community that has brought death? Where can I follow you into places of trauma to convey your healing? How can I stop bowing up and instead apologize for wrongs of the past? Where must doubling down be replaced by atonement? How can denial of racism be displaced by flourishing? How can places of death be resurrected to be places that give life?

23

Anger

The older brother became angry and refused to go in.

In the film *Legends of the Fall*, three Ludlow brothers fall in love with Susannah. The first brother, Samuel, marries Susannah. Samuel dies in war. Susannah falls in love with the second brother, Tristan, but he soon leaves. Tristan travels the world until his hair grows long enough to flow behind him when he returns home on a horse. I am not telling you who played Tristan because I want to stay focused here, but some of you already know, and I've lost you.

Finally, the third brother, Alfred, marries Susannah. Plot spoiler coming. Then again, you've had decades to watch this movie. Susannah tragically dies, and Alfred says to Tristan, "I followed all the rules; man's and God's. And you? You followed none of them. And they all loved you more. Samuel. Father. And my, even my own wife."

The elder son in the parable had followed all the rules; man's and God's. He is the model of a good young man. He does everything right. When he hears music and sees the dancing, the servant confirms what he feared was true. His father is throwing a party for that squanderer! Righteous indignation wells up like bile in his throat, and it's about to erupt.

The elder son is raging, and we begin to get the sense that he too is lost. He didn't have to leave home to lose his way. He is lost and angry in the fields nearby. He is a prodigal homebody.

Dr. Edmund Clowney tells the true story of a United States soldier missing in action during the Vietnam War. When the family could get no official word on their son, the older son took action. He flew to Vietnam and started looking for his brother. Some think he was never hurt because people on both sides of the war respected his quest. They called him simply "the brother."

In Tim Keller's *The Prodigal God*, the author and preacher reflects on Clowney's story and the elder son in the story of Jesus:

> This is what the elder brother in the parable should have done; this is what a true elder brother would have done. He would have said, "Father, my younger brother has been a fool, and now his life is in ruins. But I will go look for him and bring him home. If the inheritance is gone—as I expect—I'll bring him back into the family at my expense."[1]

Instead, the elder brother stayed home and fumed. The anger of the brother that leads to the violence of inaction reminds me of a point Cynthia Bourgeault makes about parables. They are not sweet little teachings about nice people doing nice things for nice people. They were told to make people angry! Parables are also meant to turn over our anger and see ourselves. Parables challenged the powers that be, unjust structures, and unjust people. Parables are supposed to make us look at ourselves. Looking at a parable, says Bourgeault, is like looking in a mirror.

The older brother, says Bourgeault, is a textbook example of what she calls the ego-centered operating system that with maturity and spiritual work of following Jesus can become less strident and dualistic and more unitive and deeply loving. Through the elder brother, "Jesus is asking us to look closely at that part in each one of us that insists on keeping score, that can't let go into the generosity and the blessedness," Bourgeault said.

The parable's mirror may reveal seething bitterness and fury welling up in us. *Why does my faithfulness never seem to be rewarded? What's so wrong with dutifully showing up? Why isn't that celebrated? If everyone knew what she did, they wouldn't welcome her here. Who does she think she is?*

Have you ever seen one of those two-sided makeup mirrors? If you look at the magnified side without realizing it's not a typical mirror, your face can be scary! *Prodigals* has magnified the mirror for me to begin seeing with Bourgeault's mirror. Behind that face of indignant, self-meritorious judgment is a dualistic mind that must have losers and winners, prodigals and non-prodigals, good and bad people so I know whom to trust, hate, war against. This is not the mind of Christ but the mind of the evil one and the influence of my own selfishness and ego that must change.

Bourgeault says, "The parable's concluding image—of the older son standing alone outside, refusing to join the party because he feels he has been slighted—is a vivid symbol of the way the [ego-based] operating system holds us back from joining the dance of Divine Mercy in full swing around us. If we're stuck in the ego, we can't hear the music."[2]

When we allow ourselves to look in the mirror and see the elder sibling in us, we might catch ourselves shouting, "It isn't fair," unable to hear the music and enjoy the dancing celebrations. Do you identify, as I do, with this struggle to welcome the outcast? When we have difficulty celebrating our own flesh and blood prodigals, how equipped are we to welcome prodigals who are strangers to us?

Nouwen says about the elder brother, "But when confronted by his father's joy at the return of his younger brother, a dark power erupts in him and boils to the surface. Suddenly, there becomes glaringly visible a resentful, proud, unkind, selfish person, one that had remained deeply hidden, even though it had been growing stronger and more powerful over the years."[3]

Lostness is much harder to identify in the elder son than in the younger son, says Nouwen. He did all the right things. He was obedient, law-abiding, and hardworking. He was the model son. But now the elder son doesn't seem able to step over his anger and into the party to celebrate his younger brother's return.

The most serious reason lostness is hard to fathom in the elder brother is because these feelings hit so close to home. Like the elder brother, we are trying so hard to be good, thinking our goodness can offset our sin and prodigal nature. This parable has some bad news for us if we are willing to hear it. Our efforts, while appreciated, don't make us any less prodigal than the younger brothers of the world. Elder siblings might make less visible messes but are still prodigals. I'm not trying to equivocate to the point that prodigal means nothing and everything. I'm calling us all prodigals because we are all flawed humans who have been wrong to divide up the world into prodigals and non-prodigals. Further, to ignore prodigality in each of us, then assign only the runaways of the world as prodigals is a gross misreading of how Jesus is angling the parable.

Seminary professor, friend, and author John Mark Hicks said:

> When the younger brother returned, the father welcomed him and the elder brother was enraged. The elder son knew his father's rules, but he did not know

> his father's heart. He had complied with the demands, but his heart was malformed. One can know the commands of God and even obey them precisely but still fail to know and practice the heart of God. Often, it seems, a malformed heart—a heart without compassion and mercy—hides behind precise obedience.[4]

Two decades ago, John Mark and I wrote a book titled *Down in the River to Pray*, and in the grueling writing process, I learned to appreciate the heart of Jesus in my friend John Mark, a heart with compassion and mercy that is open and confessional.

When we don't think we're a prodigal or ever have been, our ability to welcome fellow prodigals is anemic. It's hard to welcome prodigals when our boiling anger is making our own presence in the father's house rather awkward. When I look in the mirror of this parable, I wonder how much I am like the elder brother, how much I am like Alfred in *Legends of the Fall*. As Richard Rohr says in *Falling Upward*, "One character does his life totally right and is, in fact wrong; and the other who does it totally wrong ends up God's beloved!"[5] This, however, does not mean elder siblings can't also be beloved. The father runs to you, invites you, and welcomes you too, elder sibling.

What is yet to be seen is if the elder brother can process this anger. Likewise, as the parable meets our lives, can we step over our anger that shouts, "It isn't fair," and listen to some of the important questions this parable raises? One important question is, Do you really know what is fair? Whose economic scale are you using when you evaluate the world around you? Are you so sure you have done your share in every sphere of your corner of the world so that the scales of justice are on your side, that you are owed something you deserve and others you deem unworthy do not deserve? What if you could stop judging others for good?

What if you might learn to say, "I don't have to judge her," out loud to a trusted friend or in prayer? I'm not talking about merely giving someone the benefit of the doubt, because I doubt that will benefit anyone. I'm talking about considering what it means to enter a "party," a church, a friendship, a working relationship, a family reconciliation with people you are angry with and think are sinners. That's what Jesus did in real life and part of what he is alluding to in this parable.

Will you, elder sibling, step over your self-justifying anger, look yourself in the mirror, stop judging by your own earth-bound standards, and open yourself to a merciful, gracious love toward other flawed, even sinful, humans? Will you stay outside the party with the elder son, burn with envy and self-righteous judgment, and refuse to go in? Will you repent, taking on the mind of Christ, and enter the party to rejoice with fellow prodigals?

Prodigal Prayer

God, when I put on the worn-out shirt of hostility, help me see myself in the mirror and change into your best robe of gratitude, compassion, and mercy.

24

Plead

So his father went out and pleaded with him.

Author and artist Catherine Anne Lombard said she has always loved the parable of the father and two sons, yet she also struggles with something about the parable. "The story seems so male in context," Lombard said.

The father offers inheritances not to daughters but to sons. Even when the youngest son squanders property, the father throws him a party. And the father pleads with the elder son to understand and support these actions. What does the father want? The elder son to give a toast at the party like a best man?!

No mother or daughters are anywhere to be found in the story. Lombard wonders, "What would the story of the prodigal daughter be, and what would her return to the welcoming mother reveal?"

Lombard imagines a prodigal daughter today burying her talents and ambitions, running after ways to please patriarchal notions of womanhood. She tries to change her body because society does not value her as she is. She stays in loveless relationships while being abused in exchange for security and material comfort.

What would it be like for the prodigal daughter to come home? The prodigal daughter must return to her mother, for it is the mother who gave her life and must reignite her soul, Lombard says. When the daughter turns toward home and is close to the house, the mother also runs to embrace and kiss the daughter. The mother wraps the daughter in the best robe and fine shoes, and slips a ring on her finger. There will be a party for the prodigal daughter, and an elder daughter will refuse to go in.

In the parable Jesus tells, this is the second time the parent goes out to meet a child. This time it is to plead with the older child. We might assume the pleading is about the elder child coming into the party. We know the elder child has refused to go in, but there is nothing in the text that says the content of the pleading is all about partying with the family. The angry elder sibling has already decided not to attend. The pleading is about the relationships of parents and children; but so far, we do not know exactly what is being said.

The conversation may have been like the daughter who told me her sister ran away from home. Months passed, and she came home for money, clothes, and food. She left again for a long time without communicating. This was repeated many times until the daughter who stayed home pleaded with the parents to stop giving her money and to throw away everything in her sister's room so she would quit coming back to resupply.

In their sin, daughters struggle to love themselves and thus others. They must return to the mother who can bring them into wholeness again. The mother will guide the prodigal daughters to find their lost voices and regain love for their own bodies as image bearers of God.

With Lombard, I wonder why her version of the Prodigal Daughters never appears or is given voice in church liturgies but only exists in her imagination. She says the ring, the robe, and the shoes are too big and keep falling off. Lombard concludes, "I long for a liturgy that makes me free instead of one that makes me wither, one that resounds with the poetry of Jesus' own words and actions and allows me to be."[1]

Part of the parable mirror for me has been to remove the unnecessary maleness of stories. The mirror led me to be inclusive in the telling, beginning with the very title of the book not being male but for all genders. We are all prodigals. Women have their own prodigality that they must learn to see in the mirror themselves. Men have their own prodigality that they must learn to see in the mirror themselves. LGBTQ+ individuals too must look in the mirror of this parable and follow where Jesus leads.

I appreciate Lombard's take on the parable. Rather than dwelling in the Bible's overabundance of patriarchy, Lombard instead imagines freely. This chapter is an example of what I believe it means to look in the mirror of the parable, step away from my patriarchal, prodigal nature, and hand out mirrors for all people to look for themselves at what Jesus may be saying to them. The party is in progress, and in the economics of the kingdom of God's grace, there is enough for everyone. The father, the mother, the God of the Universe who created you, the Christ revealed in Jesus, and the Spirit hovering over the earth since the beginning are pleading with us who are outside the party to enter and enjoy the divine banquet for all prodigals willing to take that step in the door.

This is what parables are meant to leave open: a retelling that is challenging and not threatened by orthodoxy violations. Can you begin to imagine the parable speaking to you as a younger or older prodigal daughter?

Prodigal Prayer

Jewish mothers have always historically taught their children to pray, and Mary would have taught Jesus to pray. My mother, Charlotte, taught me to pray as a follower of Jesus.

When Mom was ten years old, she dreamed that Jesus came to her on the path to the barn at her childhood home in the Oklahoma panhandle. He raised her up six feet then dropped her back to the path. For years she believed she wasn't good enough for Jesus to pick her up and take her along. She said, "It was many years later that I learned to accept the grace and love of God."

Loving God, continue to show yourself to my mother, my sisters, my wife, my daughters, my nieces, my friends that they are beloved prodigal daughters. Your love is strong enough to pick them up—there is enough love for everyone—and welcome us all home in your divine embrace.

25

Servant

But he answered his father, "Look! All these years I've been slaving for you and never disobeyed your orders. Yet you never gave me even a young goat so I could celebrate with my friends. But when this son of yours who has squandered your property with prostitutes comes home, you kill the fattened calf for him!"

The last time I saw my dad alive, I was frustrated with him. COVID-19 shutdowns had just begun in early 2020. Dad's heart was failing in his eighty-fifth year. The church I grew up attending and he and Mom still attended was holding services online, and so was the church where I preached. I had told Dad about my online sermon, that he could watch on television. Though his heart was failing, his mind was sound till the day he died. When I asked him to watch what would turn out to be his last Sunday sermon before he died, he pulled up another sermon on the television and watched it. I left the house, and I don't know if he ever watched my sermon. My thoughts of irritation felt petty to me, and I said nothing more to Dad.

Two days later, in the middle of the night, Dad passed away. I was not there when he died. Jill and I drove back to Mom's house and cried with gathered family over Dad's lifeless body. Dad had been surrounded by family, singing him peacefully to an eternal rest with God. I am grateful for my siblings, in-laws, and mother for doing that. A few days later, because of pandemic crowd limits, Dad's funeral was outdoors and limited to family and very close friends.

In this area of affirming my work as a preacher, Dad could not be fully what I needed from him, nor did I ask directly. Earlier in life, we had already talked out our differences, and I think we just settled on not talking about it anymore. Neither could I be fully what Dad may have wanted from me. We all deal with these shortcomings of ourselves and others in a mix of healthy and unhealthy ways. I could have been more transparent with Dad and said, "It would mean a lot to me, Dad, if you'd watch my sermon." I was too stubborn to say that. I do not regret, however, being frustrated with Dad as my last interaction with him. We've loved each other more than half a century, and that moment doesn't define what our relationship was.

As it turns out, the younger son practices a speech he never gives, and the elder son who has been silent till now has a scathing speech for his father. Violence in many insidious forms lives in a space that expects everyone to love us the way we want to be loved without ever verbalizing how we want to be loved. The elder brother in us lives in the negative space of entitlement, seeing others receive what he wants and resenting it. In the elder brother there is no gratitude for the life already received, no genuine happiness for the successes of others.

The elder brother wants his goat!

That last Sunday of Dad's life, when I wanted Dad to watch my sermon, I let ingratitude get my goat. I was like the eldest brother, wanting my goat, wanting more than the much I already had. I did not want a goat like the elder brother, but I wanted the GOAT to enjoy my preaching. I think my dad was the GOAT (Greatest Of All Time) in many ways; he served in a local church, loved others, changed a community, and gave generously.

My late father was always pleading with people to follow Jesus. Mom and Dad both led me to the Lord. Dad took my hand and led me in front of the congregation. He asked me for that "good confession" of faith in Jesus Christ. Dad baptized me in the name of the Father, the Son, and the Holy Spirit for the forgiveness of my sins and to receive the gift of the Holy Spirit.

Now I sit at the desk in Dad's old office and work for the company he founded, trying to carry on—with my older (okay wiser) brother, Brent, my niece, Lauren, and hard-working employees—the values of quality, trust, and the golden rule in building homes. For years my dad has built stable, durable homes in my hometown, but he has always been most interested in building faithful lives.

On May 23, 2001, a short time after Dad had open heart surgery, he wrote a letter to everyone he could think of that he'd interacted with in the town where he'd lived for fifty years. He wrote to his construction work crew, people at his favorite restaurants, and to "Jerry and Crew and all who play the game" (of golf).

Dad wrote in his letter to all these folks,

> *Recently I told Charlotte I wanted to change my image. When you think of me, what do you think about? Is it just an old man who tells corny jokes? A guy who likes to play golf? A businessman who likes to make money? Certainly, there is nothing wrong with those things. As life goes on,*

however, we tend to think about more important things—lying on an operating table and letting doctors cut open my chest made me think more seriously about what life is truly about.

I would rather be remembered as one who loves God and loves people. Charlotte and I work with a church at the north edge of Dewey, Oklahoma, that has the motto, "The church that cares." Being on the highway, we have lots of people who stop in needing food, clothing, gasoline. We do what we can to help. We all at some time suffer from illness, depression, death of a loved one, or spiritual struggle. If we can ever be of help in these areas, we would welcome the opportunity.

Finally, our supreme goal in life is to go to heaven when we die. We want to help others go there too. There is one stunning and important question we must all ask. If I die tonight, will I go to heaven?

We love you,
Terrel and Charlotte Taylor

This letter was written by a man who had looked in the mirror and decided to change not just his image but his heart and his way of seeing others and the world. Mom and Dad noticed some people were absent from the party, and this is their pleading. Their letter was an invitation to the party that is in the divine presence of God. Maybe some friends already had given their lives to the Lord, but they wanted to name God's grace and mercy if someone had not yet found their way. The essence of my parent's letter is that the recipient of the letter is loved and someone in the flesh in their hometown is a real representation of God's love and grace.

The letter communicated a listening ear, an open table, and help in time of need.

The father in the parable also notices that the elder son is absent from the party. He leaves the party to plead with his eldest son. At this point, the elder son has chosen not to enter the party for his younger brother. The essence of the father's pleading is to reconnect his sons. Likewise, preacher Rick Atchley says both sons are offered the same love from the father. Both sons resent their father. Neither son wants the father as much as the father's stuff. Both sons feel they need to earn their father's love. Both sons break their father's heart.

"He had a son, too bad to be true. And he had a son, too good to be bearable. Both of his sons chose to put distance in the relationship. Both in their own way kept their father at arm's length," Atchley said. "He is pleading with the elder son because he longs for all the children to be back at the table. Both sons can do nothing to make the father stop loving them."[1]

The elder brother's grievance moves in a three-part parallel irony. The elder brother first portrays his own position in the household. He has worked hard, obeyed, and not been appreciated. "You never gave me even a young goat so I could celebrate with my friends," the elder brother tells his father.

The elder brother is setting up an ironic comparison between his actions and the actions of the younger brother. In contrast to his hard work, the elder brother says the younger brother has squandered family wealth. Where the elder has been obedient, the younger has been disobedient. Disobedience is personified with a vivid example of the younger brother spending family money with prostitutes. The kicker, complains the elder son, is rewarding the squandering sexual sinner with a fatted calf barbecue!

The elder brother is right. Who in their right mind would stand for such a double injustice? Hard work seems to be unrewarded;

squandering in sexual sin seems to be rewarded. The deeper irony of the story is while the younger son was lost and found, the elder son remains lost. Self-righteous condemnation of others always has a dark side of a false self that is being covered up.

How is this irony of the elder sibling's lostness and cover-up playing out in our lives today? We live in a world in which it seems so many of us have lost the way. When we get lost, there is a kind of obsession. Some are obsessed with finding their way home, back to God, to loving others. Others seem obsessed with the sins of others and staying in the state of anger and cover-up of their own faults.

This cover-up allows elder siblings to think certain people are not fit for their communities. Elder siblings want to make rules for communities, private and public, that attempt to protect an imagined pure flock of people from the polluted prodigals who they say are guilty of certain kinds of sins. Rather than have difficult conversations around sexuality and gender, for example, elder siblings wish to deny the fact that families are struggling with these issues in their churches. Elder siblings rant on social media about the degradation of morals, then indulge in pornography on a hidden tablet no one in the house knows about.

I am not above this kind of cover-up, nor have I tamed my wayward prodigal heart. How can we move from being lost siblings covering up our own sins while uncovering sins of others, to being elder siblings who realize we are fellow prodigals? Over the years, family members and friends have been my accountability partners as I confess the deadly sins of lust, gluttony, greed, sloth, wrath, envy, and pride. Being prodigal moves us again and again away from secret sins and self-righteous judgment and into a right relationship with God and fellow prodigals. James the brother of Jesus calls for confession of our own sins that heals us. James says, "Therefore confess your sins to each other and pray for each other so that you may be healed. The prayer of a righteous person is powerful and effective" (James 5:16).

I have witnessed my parents wrestling free from the act of barring people in this way from their community. The letter Mom and Dad wrote is a good example of how they displaced self-righteous judgment with forgiveness, healing, love, and life. As you can see in the stories I've been telling you, I have also been wrestling free from the condemnation racket that attempts to rank sins of prodigals. What seems to be preventing the elder son from entering the party is the false self that believes others are prodigals and he is not. The elder brother is a prodigal, too. Part of wrestling free is realizing I will always be a prodigal on my way home. I am a fellow prodigal.

Frederick Buechner in *Telling the Truth*, said of the elder brother, "The fatted calf, the best Scotch, the hoedown could all have been his too, any time he asked for them except that he never thought to ask for them because he was too busy trying cheerlessly and religiously to earn them."[2]

He. Never. Asked.

Is there something you want to ask a loved one?

26

Son

"My son," the father said, "you are always with me, and everything I have is yours."

Elias Chacour was an eight-year-old boy in 1948 when his family was displaced from their home in Palestine by Israeli militia. Elias wondered why his family was being forcibly removed from land they had farmed for generations. No longer would he climb the orange and olive trees and pick their delicious fruits.

Not only Elias but much of the world was perplexed how a United Nations vote could deed over half of Palestine to Israeli settlers. The world had compassion on Jewish people after the Holocaust, and rightly so. Zionism drove a narrative that Israel should return to biblical lands, and there was enough political will in the United States and Europe to support a diaspora of Jews returning to Palestine.

The problem was that Palestinians had been living for hundreds of years in regions that were part of the planned land transfer. On May 15, 1948, British occupation of Palestine was exchanged for Israeli occupation, and hundreds of thousands of Palestinians became refugees in exile in the Middle East.

Elias and his family were one of those refugee families in ever-shrinking Palestinian lands. In spite of being displaced and persecuted, Elias was taught the nonviolent ways of Jesus. He attended school and later a theological seminary where he became a Melkite Catholic priest. He was assigned to serve the church in a little town in Galilee called Ibillin.

Half a century later, Elias was still in Ibillin when the group I was traveling with met him at the school he founded. Like many Americans, I have for most of my life tried to understand the issues around what we often call the Holy Land. In my limited understanding shaped by religious, political, and media narratives, I thought of Palestinians as the Palestinian Liberation Organization of Yassar Arafat. I thought of Palestinians as terrorists and Israelis and their allies like the United States as their victims. Chacour confirmed that when he traveled in the United States, he was scrutinized as if he may be a terrorist. Viewing Palestinians as terrorists is a wrong, incomplete, and inauthentic narrative because it is based in stereotypes, is narrowly one-sided, and fails to take into account and hear the voices of Palestinians.

This narrative has been so in force that one person recently told me she did not realize Palestinian Christians existed. Though many Palestinian Christians live outside of the region, we met many Palestinian Christians on a tour of Palestine and Israel. I had expected to be most inspired by holy sites where Jesus walked, and no doubt those experiences met and exceeded my expectations. What upended my expectations, however, was that most of my life-changing interactions were not with holy sites but with holy people like Chacour who live in the region.

Over the years in his ministry in Ibillin, Chacour had seen injustice where non-Jewish Israeli citizens received substandard education. So he started a school for all children regardless of their religion. Chacour learned the nonviolent ways of Jesus from how his parents passed peacefully through the "Nakba," the catastrophe of Jewish settlements that has displaced Palestinians for decades.

He said to his students, "When a student joins our school, do not think of him as an enemy but a neighbor. You were not born as a Christian, Muslim, or Jew but babies in the image of God."

Students at the school call Elias "Abuna," which means father. Abuna communicates something like this: "Behave as our father, and we will behave as your children."

Abuna Chacour's life reflects the image of the father in the parable of Jesus. When the elder son refuses to enter the party, the father goes out to him. Was the father carrying a plate of fatted calf barbecue for his hungry elder son? Once again in the story, the father takes the initiative to love one of his sons.

We do not know if the elder son ate from the fatted calf or even entered the feast. This question leaves open the possibility that we can enter into the story with our own wonderment. I wonder if I would go in? Could I step over my bitterness and jealousy? I wonder, could I get over my obsession with paying more, doing more than my share?

What we do know is that the father intends the elder son to receive the same blessings as the younger son. We know this by what he says next. "My child, you are always with me. Everything I have is yours."

Barbecue in hand or not, what I hear the father saying to the elder son is full of assurance. I often find what is not said to be one of the most interesting parts of conversations. The father does not say, "I am always with you," but, "you are always with me." While pointing to the arrogance and self-meritorious judgment of elder siblings and those rejecting Jesus's openness toward sinners, Jesus still angles at the elder son's faithfulness. He is declaring that the older son is also an heir and everything the father owns belongs to the elder son as well. One important question for the elder son is the same for us. Will we as sons and daughters of a good and loving parent receive good gifts with gratitude? Or will we let comparisons, jealousy, and pride get our goat?

I was amazed at the gracious way Abuna Chacour lived his life. When we were sitting in the classroom and he was at the desk in front as our teacher, he posed a question that our research group discussed together at length. Chacour asked, "To whom does God say the land belongs?" I am still pondering this valuable question.

The question and problem are much like what the father and sons in the parable were wrestling about. Who gets the inheritance? Does God favor one nation over others? Who has squandered what? Who are the rightful heirs to the land? These are core questions around conflicting claims of land in Palestine and Israel, just as they are compelling questions around the history of land grabs in the United States.

The surprising question Chacour asked has a biblical response and life-changing implications. No scripture has ever definitively declared a particular people as owners of any sacred land. Who does land belong to then? Repeatedly Scripture says, "The earth is the Lord's, and everything in it." Israel is called a tenant, caretaker. The nations are also named as tenants and caretakers and partakers in the blessings of the land that belongs to God.

The land does not belong to us as humans. We belong to God and God's land, and in fact in the origin story of the Bible, we are people made from dirt. That's what Adam means, man made out of land or clay. Like Adam and Israel, descendants of God's people are to be caretakers of the earth. We are called to bring justice, equality, and love, not strife, greed, and bloodshed.

I wish I could tell you about many other holy people we met in Palestine and Israel, like Abuna Chacour, who are living out these values in the holy lands. I do not have space to tell the stories of faithful, courageous people like a Palestinian Quaker we met in Ramallah named Jean Zaru. You can read Zaru's story in her book, *A Palestinian Woman Speaks.*

I'll say again, walking in the paths where Jesus walked and taught was inspirational, but even more inspiring than holy sites were the holy people we met like Chacour and Zaru. They are living images of Jesus, fellow prodigals finding their way home.

The prodigal parable has no specific location setting, and we do not know exactly where Jesus was when he told the parable. He was heading to Jerusalem and had been teaching in Galilee, so he's likely somewhere in the vicinity of modern day Ramallah, where we met Zaru, when he tells the parable.

As I listened to the stories of Chacour and Zaru, the parables and other teachings of Jesus flooded my mind. I was amazed at the forgiving, loving, generous spirit that has no religious, racial, gender, ethnic, or political borders. Because of a warped view of land and possession of land, Israel and Palestine have a complex system of thirty-foot walls that divide Israeli from Palestinian territories. Zaru said even though she lives only ten miles from Jerusalem, to get there for her and other Palestinians requires hours of wait time and harassment at various Israeli military check points.

Even Bethlehem is walled off, though it is only three miles from Jerusalem. Bethlehem is mostly inhabited by Palestinians. We stayed in Bethlehem five nights and observed how difficult life is for Palestinians in occupation. The "Walled Off Hotel" showcases "the world's worst views." It is a cafe built next door to a thirty-foot wall similar to the walls the United States has built on the United States–Mexico border the past few decades.

In spite of all these divisions, when we went to Jerusalem, we saw a potent and compact expression of what people all over the region are trying to do. The generous spirit of Chacour and Zaru has spread to many Palestinian Christians, Muslims, and Israeli citizens. In Jerusalem, distracted by delicious smells and tastes of honey-dripping pastries and Turkish coffee, I nevertheless observed something beautiful. Pilgrims like us from all over the world were walking the four quarters of the city: Jewish, Christian, Muslim, Armenian.

We were led by one of our traveling companions, Father Dewayne, in prayers along the stations of the cross on the Via Dolorosa. With pilgrims from around the world, we walked this way of sorrows where Jesus was condemned, nailed to an execution device, buried, and raised from the dead three days later.

The most surprising observation I made in my brief experience of this holy city is that people who live in Jerusalem and the surrounding lands are trying harder than any outsiders can possibly imagine to live harmoniously, to flourish together through nonviolence, equality, and justice. This inclusive love has always been God's way. Humanity has not lived up to this inclusive love. The great adventure of humanity, by God's grace, is that we are prodigals who can continue to lean into this inclusive love. I can hear God saying, "My children, you have always been with me. Everything I have is yours."

I have told you about Chacour and Zaru as one way of showing how this parable can be fleshed out in different parts of the world communally. This parable is not only for personal application; it can be applied communally. So as I close how the parable of love for all prodigals can be applied to each of us as individuals as well as in communities, I declare this: No matter where in the world you live or have been raised, there is enough of God's love to go around and supply your need for mercy, grace, and compassion. There is nothing that can ever stand between you and the love of God, not even sin. Can you lean into this love of God expressed in this parable that includes you no matter where in the world you are today?

Prodigal Prayer

Dear God, our world and local communities have been flooded with cultural, political, and religious conflict. I keep forgetting you are in control and often fail to trust in you. Show me how to respond as a fellow beloved prodigal to global and local problems we face daily.

27

Rejoice

"But we had to celebrate and be glad, because this brother of yours was dead and is alive again; he was lost and is found."

Two of Kamla Fatima's sons had been missing a month when the police officer visited her home in Ganesh Talai, India. The police officer showed her a photo of a dead body by train tracks. It was her fourteen-year-old boy, Guddu, who had fallen from the train and died. Did the police officer know anything about her five-year-old boy, Saroo?

What Kamla knew was that a month ago her younger son, Saroo, had tagged along with her older son, Guddu, to find work and support the family who lived in poverty. Saroo loved his oldest brother like a father. Their father had abandoned the family a few years before. Saroo had always wanted to go with Guddu to the next city to work. His older brother had finally given in and allowed him to go.

What Kamla did not know was that the two brothers got separated at a train station. Trying to find his brother, Saroo got on a train that took him hundreds of miles across the country to Kolkata. Guddu most likely died frantically searching for his five-year-old brother, Saroo.

Kamla felt searing grief for her oldest son, Guddu, who she now knew was dead. She also felt a deep concern for Saroo, who could still be alive and lost. She had to go and find him. Kamla asked everyone in town about Saroo, when they'd seen him last, did they have any clues where he was. She made regular trips to surrounding cities to look for Saroo. The weeks and months turned into years. Though her former husband and father of her children moved two hundred kilometers away with another woman, Kamla stayed in Ganesh Talai because of the possibility that Saroo might someday come home. She stayed in the same neighborhood twenty-five years. For an excruciating 9,125 days and nights Kamla waited in hope that her lost child would someday come home.

Then one day, Saroo returned home, just as his mother had always hoped. As her son stood in front of her, Kamla was speechless. For a moment, both mother and son had to stare into one another's eyes and examine facial structures to recognize each other. As neighbors gathered around, Kamla took her adult son by the hand, and they returned to her modest home, where she called Saroo's siblings and told them, "Your brother Saroo is alive! Come and see him, he's at my house."

The story Saroo now told Kamla—how he got lost on a train as a five-year-old, was adopted from an orphanage and grew up with the Brierley family in Australia, then found his way back home at age thirty—is now told in his book, *A Long Way Home*. The book later became a movie called *Lion*.

Saroo asked about his brother Guddu. On the same day his mother learned her son was alive after twenty-five years, Saroo learned his brother had died in a tragic accident.

Even at this first meeting, Kamla told her long-lost son she was grateful to his adoptive parents, the Brierleys, for raising him in Australia. She said they had the right to call him son since they had raised him and made him the man he is today. Her only concern was that Saroo should have the very best life he could have.

The final words the father says in the parable could also be the words of Kamla when Saroo came home after twenty-five years. "But we had to celebrate and be glad, because this brother of yours was dead and is alive again; he was lost and is found."

By now in the parable of Jesus, the dogs are gnawing on the bones of the fatted calf. The story ends before we see the elder brother decide whether he will act on his father's pleas to celebrate with them. In fact, there's a past tense in the final sentence that suggests the party is already over. "We had to celebrate."

The older brother had distanced himself from his father and brother. In talking to his father about this, he had said, "Your son." Now the father, instead of saying, "my son," names him "your brother." With these word choices, he is reconnecting the younger prodigal to the elder prodigal.

Likewise, the parable may reconnect who we think is the prodigal to us as fellow prodigals. Our Creator parent pleads with us to accept as "your sister" and "your brother" those we have disowned as hopeless prodigals while labeling ourselves as faithful children. If you consider yourself a hopeless prodigal, you may find hope in recasting religious people who condemn you as "fellow prodigals" or "my elder siblings." That is the point of urging the rejoicing together—because celebration is a sign of inclusion and love.

The parable has now moved from the elder brother and the Pharisees and teachers of the law to us. The prodigal story of Jesus leaves an open question for you and me. Will you come to the party? What if we learn to rejoice with those we have labeled prodigals? Would you throw a party for those who do not fit our religious, political, moral, and racial categories as worthy of celebration?

The irony is that the older brother remains lost. It seems like Luke tells these stories in such a way so as to remind readers three times that the lost are found when Jesus is around. Jesus eats with sinners, outcasts, and prodigals. If you can accept it, you are a prodigal, and I am a prodigal, too. We're called to enter the party, to move from grumbling and missing the grace we've already received. The father says to us, "All I have is yours." With such receiving of grace, we can move to a place of channeling that same gracious gift of God to others.

Here is another connection point with the three parables Jesus tells. The coin was lost, and now it has been found. The lamb was lost, but now it has been found. Likewise, the elder brother is urged to come celebrate because "this brother of yours was dead, and is alive; he was lost, and is found."

After each of the three parables, there is a call to celebrate that should give us a clue to the meaning of the parable, the thread that runs through each. Here we can read all three celebration statements in a row. Watch how there is a move in each parable to show God, angels, and human prodigals overjoyed when the lost come home.

> And when he finds [the lamb], he joyfully puts it on his shoulders and goes home. Then he calls his friends and neighbors together and says, "Rejoice with me; I have found my lost sheep." I tell you that in the same way there will be more rejoicing in heaven over one sinner

> who repents than over ninety-nine righteous persons who do not need to repent.
>
> And when she finds [the coin] she calls her friends and neighbors together and says, "Rejoice with me; I have found my lost coin." In the same way, I tell you, there is rejoicing in the presence of the angels of God over one sinner who repents.
>
> "My son," the father said, "you are always with me, and everything I have is yours. But we had to celebrate and be glad, because this brother of yours was dead and is alive again; he was lost and is found."

This bundle of parables points to the same eternal mystery: lost people matter to God. The untold response of the elder brother leaves space that invites you and me to contemplate our own lostness. Our lostness matters to God, and it matters to God that we are found. Lost prodigals you secretly hate matter to God. The parable is not asking us to condone wayward, abusive, sinful acts of ourselves or anyone else. The parable is urging us to love and care about lost people because God does, because we are fellow prodigals on the way home, and because when lost people get found, there is great rejoicing on earth and in heaven.

Epilogue

We all are prodigals on the way home.

Three famous people were born in Kingsland, Arkansas: Bear Bryant, Johnny Cash, and Raymond Smiley. One of these men became even more famous for being my father-in-law. As a United States Marine, Smiley likes to say about his duties in Hawaii that he protected Waikiki Beach. Joking aside, I appreciate and bless my father-in-law, Ray Smiley, for his service to God and a grateful nation. Ray is a self-taught theologian who has been teaching me great humility and love since I began dating his daughter in 1985.

While I could say I most appreciate Ray and my mother-in-law, Bobbie Smiley, for the amazing daughter, Jill, they raised who has been my wife and best friend nearly four decades, there is so much I have learned from and appreciate about the Smileys.

Ray and Bobbie met in Houston where they married, bought a house in the 1960s, and still live. Bobbie was the first woman in her East Texas family to earn a master's degree. She masterfully taught generations of students at Pearl Hall Elementary School while Ray worked every refinery in Houston as a chemical engineer. Just as my parents have served for decades in one Oklahoma church, so also the Smileys have been servant leaders for decades in the same Texas church. Like my parents, my in-law parents are also known for loving and welcoming all people.

Ray took Jill to the Astrodome to watch the Astros baseball team in the era of Jose Cruz and Nolan Ryan. Turning it around, Jill recently took Ray to an Astros game at Minute Maid Park in this era of Jose Altuve and Framber Valdez. We watch the Astros many nights of the baseball season, and I'm grateful to enjoy the excitement, stories, and sheer fun of sports spectating.

I remember when I asked Ray and Bobbie for their blessing to marry Jill. They told me one thing that I will never forget: "Help each other get to heaven." Jill and I did not realize some of the hell we would go through and put each other and family members through. Ray and Bobbie were always with us, however, loving and supporting us no matter what. The way I have translated their advice over the years is that we are to live that line in the Lord's Prayer: "Your will be done on earth as it is in heaven." What this means in practice is that we are to creatively find ways locally that we can bring heavenly love to earth until God shows us somewhere else to bring it.

The Smileys model what one of my favorite theologians, Blaise Pascal, said: "Knowing God without knowing our own wretchedness makes for pride. Knowing our own wretchedness without knowing God makes for despair. Knowing Jesus Christ strikes the balance because he shows us both God and our own wretchedness."[1]

The Smileys have shown me what I have been trying to say throughout this book. We are all prodigals on the way home. The Smileys embody in their neighborhood, school, work, and church what it means to be beloved prodigals. They have always been well aware of their faults and of how much God loves us and every single human being, no exceptions. They challenged their meathead son-in-law to learn his own faults and join in being a beloved prodigal on my way home.

I find myself now in the parent-in-law position of the Smileys, learning to love new family members and be loved by them. My new in-laws have endeared themselves to me because they love, respect, and care deeply about my children. They have been generous not only to my children but to the entire family. Brendan, my son-in-law, works in professional baseball, developing young players as well as video technology to aid in coaching. He helps us see live games and occasionally get the gloves out to have a catch! In-laws give us opportunity to love as we find each other, not as we wish each other to be.

I have already written about my daughter-in-law, Sidney, but must add that she and Jacob have a baby named Samuel Ross! They are good parents, and their siblings are good aunts and uncles. Jill and I are grandparents for the first time! Family names and blessings will be passed along once more. My Grandma Grace, whom I told you about in chapter one, died the same day our oldest, Ashley, was born. We changed her middle name that day to Grace. In Uganda, mothers get named after their firstborn child with the word "Mama" and the child's name. Jill came to be known to our Ugandan friends as Mama Grace.

All this talk of in-laws and family roles is my way of reminding us about taking on a new identity. We all have changing identities and relationships of one kind or another. Taking on new roles such as neighbor, mother, father, daughter, uncle, in-law, or grandparent is a gracious mystery, a challenge, and can be great fun. New identities, roles, and expectations have a way of renewing your mind and heart. Likewise, I've challenged you to consider taking on a new identity as a prodigal, turning toward home when you've lost your way. What does taking on the identity of prodigal mean for your life? Only you will know, and you will do a better job leaning into and living this new identity than any to-do list I could give you.

There is a strong focus today in books and sermons in churches on doing. We often have little imagination for becoming something internally that people may not see but is only spiritually discerned or appreciated by God who knows our hearts. In this book, I have tried not to tell giant stories that often do not encourage more love as much as they encourage us to idolize the teller or subject of the story. Instead, I have tried to write the kind of ordinary stories of learning to love in our web of relationships that interrupt our constant "doing" and striving of the elder sibling while also confronting counterfeit confessions of young siblings.

I want to leave you with a word of grace and peace. May the grace of the Lord Jesus Christ, the love of God, and the fellowship of the Holy Spirit be with you always.

Prodigal Prayer

God, I am a prodigal, and this prodigal nature brings so much heartache and violence into the world. Thank you, Elder Sibling and Savior Jesus, for taking on a flexible identity of a Prodigal wanderer in this world. You reversed the idea of prodigals by becoming prodigious, saving love in the flesh, given completely for us. By the mystery of the Holy Spirit and the flexible identity of letting us know you as mother, father, brother, child, and lamb, please forgive the sin in me and in all humans that harms others. Bring us home and heal us. Give us the joy of the beloved who was lost and found, dead and now alive.

Acknowledgments

I want to thank you for taking the time to read my thoughts on the greatest parable Jesus ever told. I humbly request that you pass the book along by purchasing copies as gifts for your church staff, friends, neighbors, and family members. A portion of the proceeds from this book will support 1256movement.org.

My wife, Jill R. Taylor, is my faithful best friend and first editor. She saves you from having to read a lot of junk. She has always made me a better writer and preacher by speaking the truth to me with suggestions for how to improve. Jill and I both want to bring equity and make "good trouble" in environments we find ourselves inhabiting. Jill is my ride or die. We share an egalitarian marriage of lifelong love and service to our community, and for that I am so grateful. As with her own work as a leading educator, she insists we do work that is good and true. I have enjoyed her tireless support for this project.

I'm grateful to my family, my parents, Terrel and Charlotte Taylor, my in-laws, Ray and Bobbie Smiley, my grandparents on my father's side, Amazing Grace and Old Rugged Ross Taylor, my uncle Rudy Taylor, my children, Ashley, Anna, and Jacob, and their significant others, for their support, love, and humility in allowing their stories to be told. I'm grateful to Jacob for writing the foreword. Jacob, your toast is happily accepted and slurped. Like me, Jacob's middle name is Ross, after my grandpa, Old Rugged Ross. Jacob and Sidney's son, Samuel Ross Taylor, also carries on this family middle name.

Special thanks to readers Jill Taylor, Ashley Taylor, Charlotte Taylor, *Black Wall Street Times* Associate Editor Deon Osborne, Wade Hodges, and Brent Abney. Friends should not make friends read early drafts of books, but now you see how these people love me. They did a service for readers of the published book who can enjoy a smoother read because of these friends and family slogging through my half-baked thoughts. Thank you to the aforementioned readers and the following friends who took the time to say nice things about the book in spite of its flaws: Sara Gaston Barton, Andy Taylor, Jack R. Shock, John Mark Hicks, Amy Bost-Henegar, Karen L. Robu, Todd Lollar, and Leonard Allen.

To friends and family who have stood beside us in the midst of our prodigal lives and turned their faces home with us, we are so grateful. Clint and Briley Davis have been by our side, sometimes literally living next door, since 1998, and we deeply appreciate their faithful friendship and family bonds.

My friend Peggy Anderson is an author and illustrator with a compassionate heart and joyful imagination. When I shared my idea of writing a chapter about each scene in the prodigal parable, Peggy sketched scenes such as the ones in the text of the parable early in the book. I'm grateful to Peggy and her enthusiasm for this book. You can learn more about Peggy's illustrations and order her books at http://authorillustrator.com/.

Special thanks to Phillips Theological Seminary, Disciples of Christ, who were sponsors of the Palestine-Israel trip I took that you learned about in this book.

When my friend Leonard Allen left Leafwood Publishers, I was unsure of my future with publishing. Then I met the new director of Leafwood, Jason Fikes, and I knew editorial and production work was in good hands. Jason and I have a long-distance friendship as so many writers and editors do. We have met up in person many times at events and also enjoy talks on the phone about current events and things we both care about, like our families, following Jesus, and publishing. I'm grateful to Jason and the whole Leafwood and ACU Press team for taking on this book and for their deft editing. Jason's guidance ranges from naming sources I had not considered to pegging where my writing fell off a cliff edge and was not going to fly. Sometimes with my attempts at humor, he might suggest something funnier or simply ask, "Really?"—and I was off to do another rewrite.

Managing editor Mary Hardegree kept the project on task and on time. I had the audacity to ask Leafwood for the most skilled editors for my book, and Mary fits this request for the best! She is such a joy to work with and has refined the book so beautifully along with the rest of the production team. She took up the thankless task of copyediting, with formatting help from Emily Mazar, and together they covered a multitude of grammatical sins and typos! Sandy Armstrong is the best typesetting designer you will find, and I have enjoyed working with her on a dozen book projects over the years. The flaws you may find in the book are all on me. For twenty years now, Leafwood and I have been loyal and faithful to one another's missions. Duane Anderson, Director of Sales and Operations, has been the constant in this long relationship, and for him and this longevity as publisher and author, I am eternally grateful. Every writer needs good editors, sales, and production managers like the incredibly talented Leafwood team!

Special thanks to Robbie Goldman and "Renee" for offering the amazing double prodigal story from Dry Bones Denver.

The Taylor family wiener dog, Hershey, kept me company for nearly every sentence of this book, so here is one more notch in the belt of dogs as best friends.

Notes

CHAPTER 1

[1]Amy-Jill Levine, *Short Stories by Jesus: The Enigmatic Parables of a Controversial Rabbi* (New York: Harper Collins, 2014), Kindle, 10.

CHAPTER 3

[1]Thomas Heath, "How to Divvy Up the Inheritance—And Keep the Family Together," *Washington Post*, June 1, 2018, https://www.washingtonpost.com/business/economy/how-to-divvy-up-the-inheritance--and-keep-the-family-together/2018/06/01/7e6c8658-642e-11e8-a69c-b944de66d9e7_story.html.

[2]Ruth Bell Graham, *Prodigals and Those Who Love Them: Words of Encouragement for Those Who Wait* (Grand Rapids: Baker Books, 2008), Kindle, 106.

[3]Cornel West, *The Cornel West Reader* (New York: Basic Civitas Books, 1999).

CHAPTER 4

[1]Henri J. M. Nouwen, *The Return of the Prodigal Son: A Story of Homecoming* (New York: Crown Publishing, 2013), Kindle, 41.

[2]C. S. Lewis, *The Four Loves: The Much Beloved Exploration of the Nature of Love* (1960; reprint Orlando: Harcourt, 1991), Kindle, 1,685. See also Jason Lepojärvi, "A Friend's Death: C. S. Lewis' Disagreement with St. Augustine," *Sehnsucht: The C. S. Lewis Journal* 5/6 (2011): 67–80. https://www.jstor.org/stable/48580490.

CHAPTER 7

[1]Helen Branswell, "WHO: Nearly 15 Million Died as a Result of Covid-19 in First Two Years of Pandemic," STAT, May 5, 2022, https://www.statnews.com/2022/05/05/who-nearly-15-million-died-as-a-result-of-covid-19-in-first-two-years-of-pandemic/.

[2]Levine, *Short Stories by Jesus*, Kindle, 56.

[3]Cortes picked up the Iron Rule from Saul Alinsky. Mary Beth Rogers, *Cold Anger: A Story of Faith and Power Politics* (Denton: University of North Texas Press, 1990), Kindle, 64.

CHAPTER 8

[1]Lyrics quoted from the song, "Jesus Commands Us to Go," by Keith and Melody Green. Stories of the life of the Greens come from the book by Melody Green and David Hazard, *No Compromise: The Life Story of Keith Green* (Eugene: Harvest House Publishers, 2000).

[2]Philip Yancey, *Soul Survivor: How Thirteen Unlikely Mentors Helped My Faith Survive the Church* (New York: Doubleday, 2003), 44.

[3]Brennan Manning, *The Ragamuffin Gospel* (Colorado Springs: Multnomah Books, 1990), Kindle, 143–44.

CHAPTER 9

[1]John Chrysostom, *Exhortation to Theodore after His Fall*, letter 1 (Florence, AZ: St. Anthony's Greek Orthodox Monastery Press, 2019), 7–8.

CHAPTER 10

[1]Levine, *Short Stories by Jesus*, Kindle, 63.

[2]Episcopal Church, *The Book of Common Prayer and Administration of the Sacraments and Other Rites and Ceremonies of the Church: Together with the Psalter or Psalms of David According to the Use of the Episcopal Church* (New York: Seabury Press, 1979), 76.

CHAPTER 11

[1]From an interview I did for *Wineskins Magazine*, "A Revolution of Love Is Breaking Out on the Streets of Denver, Colorado" (Mar–Apr 2008).

[2]Henri J. M. Nouwen, *Life of the Beloved: Spiritual Living in a Secular World* (New York: Crossroad Publishing, 2002), Kindle, 43.

[3]Margery Kempe, *The Book of Margery Kempe*, trans. Anthony Bale (Oxford: Oxford World's Classics, 2015), Kindle, 165.

CHAPTER 12

[1]James Ford, "Lost and Found: Christian and Buddhist Parables of the Prodigal Son," *Monkey Mind* blog, November 30, 2017, https://www.patheos.com/blogs/monkeymind/2017/11/lost-found-christian-buddhist-parables-prodigal-son.html.

CHAPTER 13

[1]Ernest Hemingway, "The Capital of the World," in *The Complete Short Stories of Ernest Hemingway* (New York: Scribner's, 1987).

[2]G. K. Chesterton, *The Everlasting Man* (Dorval, Canada: Magdalene Press, 2014), Kindle, 1.

[3]Ford, "Lost and Found."

[4]Brené Brown, "The Power of Vulnerability," Ted Talks, December 2010, https://www.ted.com/talks/brene_brown_the_power_of_vulnerability?language=en.

[5]Augustine, *Confessions*, Book III, VIII.

CHAPTER 14

[1]Levine, *Short Stories by Jesus*, Kindle, 61.

CHAPTER 15

[1]Miroslav Volf, *Exclusion and Embrace: A Theological Exploration of Identity, Otherness, and Reconciliation* (Nashville: Abingdon Press, 1996), 9, 138, 158.

[2]Frederick Buechner, *Peculiar Treasures: A Biblical Who's Who* (New York: HarperCollins, 1979), 106.

[3]Bernard Brandon Scott, *Re-Imagine the World: An Introduction to the Parables of Jesus* (Santa Rosa, CA: Polebridge Press, 2001), 75–76.

[4]C. Montefiore and Loewe, from *Rabbinic Anthology*, 321, quoted in Bernard Brandon Scott, *Hear Then the Parable: A Commentary on the Parables of Jesus* (Minneapolis: Fortress Press, 1990), 117.

[5]Charles H. Spurgeon, "Prodigal Love for the Prodigal Son," a sermon preached March 29, 1891.

CHAPTER 17

[1]Max Lucado, *He Did This Just for You* (Nashville: Word, 2000), 7–15.

[2]Susan Eastman, "The Foolish Father and the Economics of Grace," *Expository Times* 117: 10, 402–5.

CHAPTER 19

[1]For source documents about death row and information about Equal Justice Initiative, see https://eji.org/reports/ and https://eji.org/issues/death-penalty/. See also https://deathpenaltyinfo.org/executions/execution-database and https://deathpenaltyinfo.org/policy-issues/innocence-database.

CHAPTER 20

[1]Volf, *Exclusion and Embrace*, Kindle, 156–66.

[2]Edward Hayes, *A Lenten Hobo Honeymoon: Daily Reflections for the Journey of Lent* (Leavenworth, KS: Forest of Peace Publishing, 1999), 77.

CHAPTER 21

[1]Nouwen, *Return of the Prodigal Son*, 12.

[2]Timothy Keller, *The Prodigal God: Recovering the Heart of the Christian Faith* (New York: Penguin Publishing Group, 2008), Kindle, 66–67.

CHAPTER 22

[1]For more information, see my Doctor of Ministry published research: Gregory Ross Taylor, "A Theological Anthropology of Black Suffering, White Supremacy, and Human Resilience after the 1921 Tulsa Race Massacre," DMin thesis, Phillips Theological Seminary, 2022.

CHAPTER 23

[1]Keller, *Prodigal God*, Kindle, 796.

[2]Cynthia Bourgeault, *The Wisdom Jesus: Transforming Heart and Mind—A New Perspective on Christ and His Message* (Boston: Shambhala, 2008), 33–35, 49.

[3]Nouwen, *Return of the Prodigal Son*, 71.

[4]John Mark Hicks, *Searching for the Pattern: My Journey in Interpreting the Bible* (Self-Published, 2019).

[5]Richard Rohr, *Falling Upward: A Spirituality for the Two Halves of Life* (San Francisco: Jossey-Bass, 2011), xxi.

CHAPTER 24

[1]Catherine Anne Lombard, "The Prodigal Daughter," *The Furrow* 53, no. 7/8 (July–Aug. 2002): 438–40.

CHAPTER 25

[1]Rick Atchley has preached on the prodigal in many places and one version of this sermon he preached at his home church in Ft. Worth is Rick Atchley, "Father and Sons," in "The Good, The Bad, and The Ugly" sermon series, https://soundcloud.com/thehillschurch/the-good-the-bad-and-ugly-8?in=thehillschurch/sets/the-good-the-bad-and-ugly-by-rick-atchley.

[2]Frederick Buechner, *Telling the Truth: The Gospel as Tragedy, Comedy, and Fairy Tale* (San Francisco: HarperCollins, 1977), 69.

EPILOGUE

[1]Blaise Pascal, *Pensées*, translated with an introduction by A. J. Krailsheimer (Harmondsworth: Penguin Books, 1966), 87.